KANT'S
CRITIQUE OF PURE REASON

KANT'S
CRITIQUE OF PURE REASON
A Reader's Guide

JAMES LUCHTE

continuum

Continuum International Publishing Group
The Tower Building   80 Maiden Lane
11 York Road   Suite 704
London SE1 7NX   New York, NY 10038

www.continuumbooks.com

© James Luchte 2007

British Library Cataloguing-in-Publication Data
A catalogue record for this book is available from the British Library.

ISBN-10: HB: 0-8264-9321-1
PB: 0-8264-9322-X
ISBN-13: HB: 978-0-8264-9321-7
PB: 978-0-8264-9322-4

Library of Congress Cataloging-in-Publication Data
A catalog record for this book is available from the Library of Congress.

Typeset by Servis Filmsetting Ltd, Manchester
Printed and bound in Great Britain by
MPG Books Ltd, Bodmin, Cornwall

For Tamara, Zoe, Soren and Venus

CONTENTS

CONTENTS

PREFACE

In the following Reader's Guide, I will set forth a comprehensive and accessible companion to the *Critique of Pure Reason* (1781/1787), which is arguably the most important work of philosophy in the last two centuries. Like the works of Plato, Aristotle and Descartes, the criteria for significance can be seen to lie in two distinct factors. On the one hand, a philosophical work or project exhibits significance in its ability to not only overcome the works of the past, but also to incorporate such legacies into a work of a higher unity. A great philosophy will never grow out of a mere rejection of the past, but instead through an appropriation and transcendence of a heritage which allows the thinking of the past to be able to speak anew to a different time and place in the historicity of life and thought.

On the other hand, a philosophy of significance will not only appropriate the works of the past for the needs of the present, but will also, in its own liberation from the past, lay the ground for philosophies of the future. Moreover, it is a testament to the power and depth of a new articulation of philosophy that it cannot simply be brushed aside with the first or second (or third, etc.) wave of criticisms, but remains as a point of reference for all, or, most, subsequent ventures of thought. Indeed, such a point of reference, as we can see from many examples, could be that of an archetypal problem, such as Zeno's paradoxes, which allows for the rehearsal of a range of critical exercises. However, Kant's *Critique of Pure Reason* is significant not only in that it provides the student with an intellectual *topos* of criticism and refutation.

On the contrary, the first *Critique* has so revolutionised philosophical method and expression that its final status as a work of philosophy is as yet *undecided*. One could contend that Kant's transcendental philosophy, taking into account his other works in the period of the Critical Philosophy, laid the foundation for every major philosophical movement in the past two centuries (even if that foundation was only the negative one of a rejected premise or perspective). It is in this way that Kant's philosophy has become a place of intersection of the past, present and future of philosophical thinking, from the ancient, the medieval, and the modern eras to the tumultuous philosophies of the nineteenth and twentieth centuries. And moreover, it is clear that with the common foundation stone of Kantianism in the opposed movements of Analytic and Continental philosophies in our current era, the legacy of Kant will continue not only to provide the ground and context for prevailing thought but will also develop and mutate across the oncoming centuries of European and World history.

NOTE ON THE TEXT

The translation which will be the main source for this *Reader's Guide* will be: Immanuel Kant, *Critique of Pure Reason*, trs. Norman Kemp Smith, St. Martin's Press, New York, 1929.

The importance of this translation lies in its unabridged presentation of the First (A) and Second (B) Editions of the *Critique of Pure Reason*. References to this translation are given in the text as NKS followed by the relevant page number. Further references to the A and B Edition page numbers are given where appropriate.

While it will be necessary to consult the primary text for a successful reading of this Reader's Guide, I will not insist on the Kemp Smith translation. A tradition has grown up around Kantian translation which has made it possible for a standardisation of the basic form of Kant's texts to such an extent that the translations have become relatively uniform. This is even the case with the many Internet translations of his works which have become increasingly available. A list of such resources is included in the Guide to Further Reading. Regardless of the translation, in a written work students should cite the edition, chapter, section and page number (or URL where applicable, with date and time of access) of the translation used.

CHAPTER 1

CONTEXT

KANT CHRONOLOGY AND BIOGRAPHY

Kant Chronology

1724 22 April, born in Königsburg, East Prussia, to a pietist family
1734 Enters Collegium Fredericianum to study theology and classics
1737 Mother dies, but remains a life-long inspiration to Kant
1740 Enters University of Konigsburg to study mathematics and physics
1746 Completes study and is employed as a private tutor for nine years. Father dies
1755 Masters degree, lectures for the next fifteen years as a Privatdozent
1766 Appointed under-librarian
1770 Appointed to Professor of Logic and Metaphysics
1781 *Critique of Pure Reason*
1783 *Prolegomena to any Future Metaphysics*
1785 *Groundwork for the Metaphysics of Morals*
1788 *Critique of Practical Reason*
1790 *Critique of Judgment*
1792 Censored in a Government crackdown for his religious doctrines and forbidden from teaching and writing on religious matters by Frederick William II
1793 *Religion within the Limits of Reason Alone*
1794 Withdraws from society but continues to lecture
1795 Limits lectures to once weekly
1797 Retires from university

King Frederick William II dies, which effectively annuls the
ban on his religious writing and teaching
The Metaphysic of Morals
1798   *Anthropology, Considered from a Pragmatic Viewpoint*
1804   February 12, dies in Königsburg

Biography

It is well known that Kant maintained a life-long habitation in
Königsberg, and as he matured, practised a legendary punctuality
and reticence. There are tales that others would set their clocks by
his early morning walks. He is said to have been, however, in his early
years as a lecturer, a reveller with extensive social contacts, would
dine often with others, and was friendly (for a while) with other
thinkers, one being Hamann, perhaps one of the most controversial
philosophers and theologians of the day. Yet it is also said that as
Kant advanced in years, even though still young, he became more
and more withdrawn due to the heavy load of his philosophical projects. In fact, there has been much speculation about what is
regarded as the paradoxical life of Kant, who never travelled more
than forty miles from his birthplace, but who articulated such global
philosophical ambitions which are still with us today. And, such
ambition was not merely about space and extent, or territory, but
was more intensely concerned with time, and primarily with the
future, with the anticipation and legislation of that nebulous
unknown. However, there seems to lurk an unstated assumption in
this narrative, and it is this assumption which breathes life into the
paradox.

The assumption is simply a re-statement of the paradox, or, in
other words, it is merely an assertion. The question is begged as to
the compatibility of the facticity of his lived provinciality and his
intellectual and cultural cosmopolitanism. While his apparently
strange reluctance to travel may be more fodder for the mills of the
psychoanalysts, there does not seem to be any inherent incompatibility between these positions, as possibilities. Indeed, it could rea-
sonably be argued, from the perspective of Kant's 'Copernican
Revolution', that, since the world – the web of representations –
revolves around the transcendental subject, the mere accumulation
of empirical representations does not make for a life of knowledge
and autonomy, or, that one need not *travel to know*. It is after all,
Kant could suggest, merely a matter of taste. With the dissolution

of the paradox, to his satisfaction, we are confronted with the raw facticity of Kant amid his lifeworld. From out of this facticity, we may divine, as Nietzsche attempts in *Philosophy in the Tragic Age of the Greeks*, an intimation of his 'personality', or, as Heidegger will suggest, his 'commitments', 'understanding' and 'mood' amidst a thrown, temporal existence.

In the wake of the diminishing stars of pure philosophy and objectivity (especially in light of twentieth-century events), the question of the relation between the life and work of a philosopher becomes unavoidable, though by no means primary. Whether he liked it or not, Kant was born, lived and died, and it is from out of the artefacts of his lived existence and the testimony of others that we begin to interpret the meaning or significance of 'Kant'.

In the first instance, we know of Kant's observed habits and his involvements with respect to the various historical phases of his life (a phenomenology of ageing) as a student, tutor, privatdozent, professor, retired, etc. We also know that each day he would read widely and write for hours on end, constantly revising and rewriting individual sentences and sections. He was a very prolific writer, and a deep and complex philosophical thinker. What snakes through all of these aspects is the consistency of Kant and his concern and need for a *topos* of security for his life and work. It should be some solace to the perplexed reader of the first *Critique* that Kant not only wrote, but also lived, his philosophy. And it could be argued that the strict criteria of his philosophy and the strictness of his practical life mirror one another. Yet, it would be a distortion to take from this that Kant was merely obsessed with control and order for its own sake. Indeed, it would not even matter if we made the utilitarian argument that his stable situation allowed him to not only be so prolific, but also to undertake such immense philosophical labours, the fruits of which are still prominent in the contemporary era. What is significant is rather that this writing articulates the notions of respect, freedom, autonomy and self-legislation, in such ways that would not only be well defended against the onslaughts of rationalism, empiricism, monism and materialism on the horizon, but would also express his *ascetic* philosophy of life. In other words, for Kant, it is self-mastery that makes freedom possible. For Kant, any conception of 'freedom' which is grounded upon materialistic interests, strategies, or, upon contingency, is an illusion. Authentic freedom is an autonomy which is not only free from the heteronomy of interest and particularity, but, as a self-naming, is also a positive obedience to the self-given moral law, a duty of self-limitation, self-legislation, with respect to other rational beings. This is not the external imposition by an occupying power, but a determination of the Will (*Willkür*) by reason (*Wille*), which as self-determination, self-legislation, intimates a state of freedom.

Nothing is known of Kant's romantic or sexual life. Indeed, if we can tell anything from his writings on marriage and sexuality, in which he states that the only acceptable sexuality occurs within legal matrimony, we would be forced to conclude that he had no sexual interaction with any other human being at all, since anything of this nature – outside of marriage as a familial contract – would be an objectification of the person as a thing to be consumed and used for pleasure. Neither would Kant countenance lying. He likewise condemns prostitution, as he would casual sex, or, unmarried co-habitations or other types of sexual relationships. And while we have dispelled the paradox which would seem to forbid anyone not living in a cosmopolitan metropolis from the possibility of significant thought, we can nevertheless draw attention to Kant's stated positions, and by implication, comment upon the limits of his lifestyle, with respect to the relevance of his rigid strictures upon life, upon others, who may not agree with his maxim, but regard his universalism as a mere opinion. Indeed, the severance between his non-sensualistic, a-temporal, unimaginative 'practical' philosophy and factical lived existence has been a major flashpoint in the criticism of Kant's deontological moral philosophy (ethics). There have even been attempts to show, despite Kant's own view's, that notions of freedom, autonomy and self-legislation entail the possibility of two autonomous persons entering into an agreement or arrangement for the exchange of sexual pleasures without violating the moral law of respect. Co-habitation would be an obvious example here. Prostitution would of course be more problematic, as it involves the commodification of the sexual body. At the very least, it is in such a context that the life of a philosopher would become relevant if his own private opinion, concealed as a maxim of moral reason, would seek to establish itself as the universal and necessary truth, even if only in a practical sense. To this extent, a consideration of his life allows us the means by which to separate the private from the essential and to begin to think for ourselves.

At the same time, Kant's thoughts on religion were indeed radical, but are in no way inconsistent with his ascetic opinions upon sexuality. For Kant, religion should be like sexuality – confined within the domain of the moral law. His radicality, one that would have put even a Luther to shame, was the elimination of the *corpus* of religion. Indeed, as we will see below, Kant, in his distinction between phenomenon and noumena, and in his 'Critique of All Theology', had already pointed the way toward a radical deconstruction of religious dogma and practice. In fact, nothing more is required than respect for the moral law. Of course, if other accessories, prayer, church-going, a bible, even other religions than Christianity, can lead to such a respect, then they should be, for Kant, tolerated as useful, though ultimately dispensable, ladders to be thrown down once the destination has been reached.

But, again, we are brought back to the question of Kant's personality. He is very Platonic in his distrust of the body and of desire. He is radical in his trivialisation of religion, which to some, would lead to questioning his commitment to matrimony. If practical reason is to be practical, it must be able to be apprehended amid 'real life'. In each situation, we are confronted with issues of respect, autonomy, pleasurable heteronomy, etc. And, it is in such situations that the meaning of the moral law must be determined and self-legislated. Yet, and this is where there must be development in the interpretation of Kant, we must attempt to disentangle Kant's own reticence in the face of the sea of existence – along with his construction of autonomy – and to attempt to set forth a Kantian notion of freedom which can stand not only the sometimes suffocating intimacy of lived existence, but also, *actual* moral dilemmas and the historicity, or genealogy, of *mores*, morality, *ethos* and ethics.

In this critical light, Bataille, in his *Theory of Religion*, pays homage to Kant by entitling Part Two, 'Religion within the Limits of Reason'. In this short work, Bataille situates the dominion of reason, and specifically of economic reason, in a historical juxtaposition with the archaic economy of the Gift. Bataille traces a notion of the *sacred* that exceeded reason, which through sacrifice externalised the factical violence of existence in a ritual which consisted in the destruction of the 'useful'. In this act, the transcendental dimension of existence is disclosed as the *topos* of the useless. With the expulsion of sacrifice from the modern rational economy, violence, for Bataille, becomes externalised in the form of class oppression and war. It is in this way that Kant is pulled off his safe island and is made to swim in the sea of historicity. The safe island of Königsberg cannot protect him from the storm which will come, as for instance, in his censoring by the King of Prussia. Some may consider his *Religion within the Limits of Reason Alone* a partial retraction of his views with his claim not to be a theologian. Yet, his resistance is quite obvious as his radical positions upon religion obtain never repeated clarity of expression. This work, while demonstrating the adaptability of critical philosophy, can however be seen as an ambiguous last act of defiance and resignation, which foreshadowed his eventual withdrawal from society.

BETWEEN THE REVOLUTIONS: THE AGE OF CRITICISM AND ENLIGHTENMENT

In this section, I will lay out the political, cultural and philosophical context of the *Critique of Pure Reason*. I will move beyond a mere contextualisation of the work, and will reflect on its direct and indirect influence upon the context of its emergence. I will exhibit Kant's specific involvement in the German Enlightenment, and his concerns with broader European and World events, such as the American Revolution. It could also be suggested that Kant had an almost prophetic engagement with the future of European and World history with such works as *Perpetual Peace* (1795), in which is articulated for the first time the idea of a 'League of Nations'. In this light, I will pay special attention to his own distinction between a private and public intellectual with respect to his own life and work.

It is certain *in retrospect* that the *Critique of Pure Reason* was not merely a child of its times, but is, as Nietzsche wrote of his own work, an untimely, or creative work, one which influenced the inauguration of a novel era in the political, cultural and intellectual destiny of Western history. However, at the time of its publication, such a destiny was not so clear to either Kant or his contemporaries. As I will detail below, this work, which took over ten years to write, was seen by its author as an attempt to mediate and transcend the stalemate between the rationalism and empiricism of his contemporaries. As with many attempts to perform such an ambitious feat, neither of the combatants of this great divide were satisfied with Kant's labours. On the one hand, rationalists, such as Mendelssohn, declared that

Kant had 'destroyed everything'. For Mendelssohn, Kant had given far too much ground to the empiricists, and especially to the sceptic Hume, in the curtailment of knowledge within the horizons of *possible experience*. On the other hand, empiricists (or at least anti-rationalists), such as Jacobi, felt betrayed by Kant in his defence of the 'authority of reason'. Increasingly critical of his earlier affinity to Wolffian rationalism, Kant was seen by many as a synthetic thinker who was guided by an historical and empirical approach (like Herder) to knowledge. It was in this light that the *Critique of Pure Reason* came as a shock to many who already had their own reasons to distrust Reason.

However, it would be difficult to understand the intensity of the reactions to the First *Critique* without an examination of the historical, political and cultural context of its emergence, that of the German Enlightenment and of the European Enlightenment more generally. It is interesting that in battles still being waged today between modernists and traditionalists, Kant's name remains at the heart of the discussion. Indeed, Kant's career as an authoritative philosopher could be said not only to span the historicity of this protracted war, but also to be intertwined with its central question of freedom. The specific flashpoint that occurred in Kant's own era, as we will see in more detail below, was the 'Pantheism Controversy' between Lessing (and Mendelssohn) and Jacobi (and Hamann). The issue was Lessing's alleged 'Spinozism'. It would seem unclear how such a philosophical dispute could have had such dramatic cultural and political implications, if we did not take into account the peculiar position that Kant had sought to occupy not only with respect to this controversy, but also in the German enlightenment per se. The charge of 'Spinozism' had a particularly sharp edge in the relatively provincial 'Germany' at the time. Still predominantly rural and unaffected by the great scientific, political, economic, cultural and technical revolutions elsewhere on the Continent and in Britain, 'Spinozism' signified a radical usurpation by Reason of traditional ways of thinking, of piety. And, despite the fact that Spinoza had identified God and the World, the status given to Reason to disclose this fact, amounted to, for Jacobi, a variation of atheism. His brand of empiricism, like that of Hamann, was that of revelation and faith, and such a pantheistic Reason, seeking to throw light on the dark recesses of human belief, was seen as an ominous threat. Thus, when Kant came down on the side of Mendelssohn, it was seen as a betrayal by Jacobi.

What was at stake, however, was not the contest of a mere 'Glass Bead Game', conducted in the solitude of Castalia, as described in Hermann Hesse's novel *Magister Ludi*. In this period of 'German' history, philosophy had a direct impact on politics and culture, and could be seen as a political activity. After decades of religious warfare across Europe, Enlightenment philosophers promised an era of peace and knowledge in the elevation of reason over all aspects of life, the nation-state, culture, science and religion. The 'Age of Reason' had transfigured into the 'Age of Criticism' in which, as Kant himself had declared in the Introduction to the *Critique* everything would be put under scrutiny. However, for Jacobi and others, the fruits of Reason were seen to be, as Baudelaire would lament some decades later, the flowers of evil. There was, of course, the English Revolution, and its child, the American Revolution, which were seen to be acts of violence enacted in the name of Reason. It was not that the 'rational is real, and the real, rational', as Hegel would later declare, but that the real had to be made rational. For the revolutionaries, such violence was a necessary evil, and one that was the lesser of two evils. The hegemony of religious authority in alliance with the absolutist state and the military was seen by the Enlightenment philosophers as a state of political, social and moral servitude. In this light, the disappointment of Jacobi, his feeling of betrayal in the controversy, could be questioned since, it seems, Kant's cards were already on the table. And, while such rationalist leanings became even more pronounced with the 1787 revisions (as we will see below), Kant was clearly on the side of the Enlightenment, even if his version was characterised by moderation and pragmatism. Yet, one need only look two years after the Second Edition of the *Critique* to witness one of the most profound rationalist social experiments in the French Revolution. For most, this is the archetypal event in the inauguration of modernity. For others, the vast minority in the contemporary world, this event, if not problematic, could be questioned as to its status as an event of freedom. In order to understand Kant's own possible culpability in the profound violence of this revolution, it would be illuminating to examine his own understanding of the Enlightenment, especially as it relates to the political sphere.

In his 1784 essay, 'What is Enlightenment?', Kant lays out his own distinct variant of the Enlightenment with the following declaration:

Enlightenment is man's release from his self-incurred tutelage. Tutelage is man's inability to make use of his understanding without direction from another. Self-incurred is this tutelage when its cause lies not in the lack of reason but in the lack of resolution and courage to use it without direction from another. *Sapere aude!* Have the courage to use your own reason! – that is the motto of the enlightenment.[1]

It is significant, in this opening statement, that Kant would locate the heart of the Enlightenment in the self, and in the courage and resolution of the self to 'use his own reason'. In this way, it is not reason that is to be demonised, it is to be seen as that which becomes corrupted when it is either not used (or not used properly) or when it is used under the direction of another. This clearly points to Kant's own notion of autonomy, and this can be seen in the present context on three different levels: philosophical, cultural and political. On the first level, Kant, as we will see in more detail below, has come to regard both sides of the battle as a form of tutelage. In both cases, rationalism and empiricism, the freedom or autonomy of the self is denied. Rationalism is seeking to throw light on the mysteries of faith, but for the advocates of revelation (empiricists), it has in fact destroyed the moral basis of freedom, and the freedom that is at the heart of morality. Spinozism threatens to swallow everything into its voracious reason, even the practical matters of morality and ethics. In this light, Jacobi should have been honoured by Kant's limitation of reason to *make room for faith.* On the other hand, Kant felt that empiricism also denied the autonomy of the self in its rejection of an *a priori* condition for knowledge. For Kant, contrary to many even today, did not think that the essence of science lay in empiricism, but in the organisational framework of such knowledge, in its method. On the second level, the opposing rules of reason or revelation in culture, and in this case, specifically religious culture, make their own encroachments upon the autonomy of the person. A rationalist culture would seek to root out 'superstition', myth, and in the manner of Plato, poetic revelation, whether religious or bohemian. A revelationist culture, especially the type that had existed in Christendom, would continue to deny the free pursuit of knowledge in science and the baroque experimentation in culture which was characteristic of the Enlightenment. In both cases, the autonomy of the self in a person's desire to pursue his or her own truth and to express such truth would be curtailed. At the third level, that of the political, we can see Kant's most explicit contribution. For while he clearly stood on the side of the political events across the ocean, and later regarded the French Revolution as an experiment in Reason, it is unclear whether he truly supported these events in their deployment of violence for allegedly rational ends. For Kant, violence for political ends is a violation of the Categorical Imperative and thus of the autonomy and freedom of the individual. On the mundane level, even belonging to a political party may be seen by Kant to infringe on the autonomy of the individual. More pointedly, the use of violence against other individuals for the sake of rational ends would be a clear violation of ethics or true morality, but would also seem for Kant to be a flagrant self-contradiction, unless of course if one regarded (as did the empiricists, et al.) reason as irretrievably wed to violence. Kant chose the middle path of the limitation of Reason in order to preserve the *topos* of moral autonomy which, for him, was the original basis for the pursuits of reason in the first place.

What is perhaps most striking, however, in all of this is Kant's statement that our tutelage is self-incurred. It is our own cowardice to think for ourselves, rather than the routine directions from another, that lies at the root of our deficiency in freedom. The responsibility for our freedom or unfreedom at the end of the day lies only with ourselves. However, this is not a call to arms, but a daring to know. Kant felt that we must respect the moral law and lawfulness *as such* and that our attempt to make the existing law more in tune with reason and freedom must be undertaken as private individuals in the dissemination of ideas. He would acquiesce to the strictures on his role as a public intellectual with respect to his teaching, which became all too apparent after his censure by the newly ascendant regime after the death of Frederick the Great. For instance, Kant admits that his *Religion*, to this day still a very radical book, does not claim to be that of a public, but of a private intellectual, looking at religion from a philosophical point of view. Yet, despite Kant's prudence, he was still able to set forth his doctrine of autonomy, advocating change through the use of reason, and not violence.

OVERVIEW OF KANT'S OTHER MAJOR WORKS

In the following, I will set forth a brief description of the significance of an array of other works by Kant which have a direct bearing upon the *Critique of Pure Reason* and the critical project of Transcendental Philosophy as a whole. Kant wrote numerous works before his so-called Critical period, yet it is widely recognised that his *Inaugural Dissertation* of 1770 was the first mature expression of his philosophy, and one that would remain consistent throughout his following works. In addition to this text, we will also consider the other two *Critiques* and three smaller works, *Prolegomena to any Future Metaphysics* (1783), *Groundwork to a Metaphysics of Morals* (1785) and *Religion within the Limits of Reason Alone* (1793) which were written for a more popular audience.

Inaugural Dissertation: On the Form and Principle of the Sensible and the Intelligible World (1770)

Of all of his early works, it seems that Kant regarded only the *Inaugural Dissertation* as worthy of publication. However, despite the relative obscurity of his so-called pre-Critical works, it is this text which can be regarded as both the fulfilment of his earlier work, between the years 1746 and 1770, and, also, as a transition to a philosophical method and expression which is distinctly his own. The influence of Leibniz and Leibnizians such as Wolff is clearly evident in these works, and many of the problems and issues with which he deals are part and parcel of the legacy of his initial teachers. Yet, with the *Inaugural Dissertation*, Kant begins to cast a critical eye upon that which he sees as an inherent confusion between the sensible and intelligible domains of philosophical inquiry. In this way, by seeking to elucidate the differentiation between these domains, he steps upon new ground which would lead, over the next eleven years, to the *Critique of Pure Reason*.

And, in a manner similar to the latter work, Kant seeks to distinguish between the finite limits of human knowledge and the domain of the things themselves. Indeed, these limits are not a weakness of the mind or a distortion of the senses (of the logical confusion held by the Wolffians), but an indication that there are not only sensible and intelligible things which are radically distinct, but also sensible and intelligible modes of cognition which are also inherently distinct. He is quite clear that the concepts of the intellect are not abstractions from sensible things, but are known, as with *moral* concepts, by the intellect directly (if not clearly). In this way, for Kant, metaphysics can be defined as the 'principles of the use of pure intellect'. He furthermore states that the preliminary work that must be undertaken, before metaphysics proper, is, as the task of the *Inaugural Dissertation*, the clear differentiation of the sensible and intelligible domains, or, foreshadowing the First *Critique*, the phenomenon and noumenon. He writes: 'For here the disagreement between the sensuous and intellectual faculties ... indicates nothing except *that the abstract ideas which the mind has received from the intellect can often not be followed out in the concrete and converted into intuitions.*'[2]

The distinction is further elaborated, also intimating the later statements of the First *Critique*, as between the receptivity of sensibility (of space and time) and the spontaneity of the intellect (concepts). However, as we will also see emerge in the First *Critique*, this receptivity of sensibility is accompanied by a formal element which organises this sensibility into appearance. We will of course see this more clearly in space and time as the forms of intuition. Kant furthermore speaks, in a clear indication of a central method in the Critical Philosophy (especially in the Antinomies), of the necessity of a *respect* between the two faculties of knowledge and a self-limitation of each to its respective realm. However, it would be just as surely stated that the *Inaugural Address* does not anticipate every development and innovation of the First *Critique*, nor the level of sophistication that was to be the fruit of Kant's so-called 'silent decade'. One such missing idea, of course, is *apperception* and its transcendental unity, which, though disputed as to its meaning, becomes the central principle of transcendental philosophy. What we gather from the *Inaugural Address* is the clearing of new ground, a new *topos*, beyond the Wolffians, from which would emerge not a mere differentiation of the sensible and intelligible domains, but what Kant would set out as a new metaphysics, or a new approach to metaphysics, regarded as a science.

Prolegomena to Any Future Metaphysics (1783)
Two years after the publication of the first edition of the *Critique of Pure Reason*, Kant published a work '. . . not for the use of pupils but of future teachers', and it is to a great extent an explication of the principles and topics of the First *Critique*. The *Prolegemona*, as Kant explains, is undertaken in an analytic manner, as opposed to the synthetic method of his *magnum opus*. He directly examines the question of the possibility of the pure sciences, such as mathematics and physics, and traces each of their conditions of possibility within

the horizons of his own *new* metaphysics. While the analytic re-articulation of the First *Critique* would, as Kant suggests, provide the teacher with an organised and concise description of the entirety of the Critical Philosophy, the *Prolegomena* is more than just a propadeutic manual or compendium, as was Hegel's *Logic*. Indeed, this was Kant's first chance to respond to the critics of the *Critique of Pure Reason*, and its power lies in the ability to analytically trace the very possibility of science to his new philosophy. It is in this way that a new approach to metaphysics was set forth over against the rationalists and empiricists of his day. To the former, whose concepts could never step out into the world, and to the latter, who could not assure us of any certainty or universality, he expressed a transcendental idealism which served as the bridge between the previously severed realms of sensibility and the concept in his doctrine of transcendental apperception and imagination.

Groundwork to a Metaphysics of Morals (1785)

Published two years after the *Prolegomena* and three years before the *Critique of Practical Reason*, the *Groundwork* is the first *sustained* articulation of Kant's moral philosophy. I emphasise 'sustained' in light of the fact that Kant intimated much of his moral philosophy, though not exhaustively, in the First *Critique*.[3] Organised in a similar analytic manner as the *Prolegomena*, the *Groundwork* seeks to clearly set forth the supreme principle of morality in the Categorical Imperative. In its three sections, Kant moves along a path from 1) ordinary rational knowledge of morality to its philosophical conception, 2) from popular moral philosophy to a metaphysics of morals, and finally from the latter to 3) a critique of practical reason. In each step along the way, he seeks to discover the conditions and meaning of the 'supreme good' or the 'good will'. For Kant, such a good will belongs to an autonomous subject who respects the moral law as its duty. Once again, this work is more than a propadeutic. It contains direct criticisms of the moral theories of rationalists and empiricists, who, Kant contended, could offer only a hypothetical imperative for morality. In the absence of that which he would characterise as universality and necessity, these moral theories were, for Kant, not in fact moral at all. Moreover, as we have seen, and will see in more detail below, both the rationalists and the empiricists lack his own notion of autonomy, which he regards as the basis for the free will, and thus, of any true morality.

Critique of Practical Reason (1788)

As we will ascertain from our consideration of the Third Antinomy below, there exists, for Kant, a *causality of freedom*, which in its *act*, is the transcendental ground for the series of representations. This causality is active *amidst*, and *as* the noumena. Yet, these are not the Platonic Ideas and the Music of Schopenhauer, who claimed that an insatiable will was at the heart of all things. Nor, is it any of the primal beings which were posited by Fichte and Schelling. Moreover, the noumena is not the result of a synthesis of the thesis and the antithesis, as it was with Hegel. For Kant, while the domain of the noumena is beyond the jurisdiction of theoretical reason, it is not therefore outside the dominion of reason itself.

Indeed, that which is distinct in Kant's approach to the noumena is his deontological approach to these things themselves. From the standpoint of the new metaphysics, it would be a transgression of the horizons of possible experience to attribute substantiality or being to the noumena, in the way which would be appropriate in the context of the First *Critique* with respect to the phenomena. Instead, in the Second *Critique*, published a year after the Second Edition of the First *Critique*, we could venture to suggest that Kant regards the noumenal dimension as a way of 'being' and 'acting' by reason which is not governed by the criteria of theoretical ontology, of time, space and causality. In this way, *practical* reason directly determines the Will, and, contrary to Schopenhauer, is not concerned with the traditional metaphysical question of the substantial core of the world, but with the practical affairs of existence in their relation to what Kant calls the *moral* law.

A significant indication of the meaning of the ethical or true morality for Kant is his explicit elimination of imagination and empirical interest from any criteria which would be used to construct a viable moral theory. And, while Heidegger may cry foul in the face of the elimination of temporality from the Second *Critique*, we can readily understand the reason why Kant seeks to place his investigation of moral reason under the sign of the eternal, as Cassirer emphasised on more than one occasion. In order for the noumenal realm to have a character which is distinctly its own, it must be, we have seen, differentiated from the realm of the phenomenon. In this way, true morality cannot be concerned with questions of expediency, consequences, of reward or punishment, or, even of feeling with respect to the justice of an action. If any of these empirical factors intervenes in the practice of moral judgment, then the judgment itself is flawed and cannot be considered to be truly moral or ethical. Indeed, for Kant, true morality consists only in obedience to the moral law, which he designates as *duty*.

Kant has often been criticised for advocating a formalistic, rigid and unworkable theory of morality, a charge which becomes most manifest in the question of competing duties. However, it will be possible to understand the meaning of his notion of the ethical by examining his advocacy of a causality of freedom. If there is to be such a causality, there must be a *topos* amid which it can *be*. We have already set forth the title of this 'place' as the noumenal realm. And we have seen the general character of this realm through the, at first, negative elimination of temporality, imagination and sensation. Yet, Kant seeks to describe a positive sense of this realm in his notion of *autonomy*. As we can see from the etymology of this term, the state of positive freedom is that of being self-named (auto-nomy), to be able to determine oneself. The nexus of causation is a grand example of everything causing and effecting everything else. Each object as a representation gains its significance through its relation with an innumerable series of other representations, or objects. This realm of causation, of time and space, in which each is named or determined by an other, Kant entitles *heteronomy*. In this light, autonomy, as the citadel of true freedom, cannot be characterised by means of the phenomenal chain of deterministic causality. It must instead exist in a differing realm which is that of a respect for the moral law for no other reason than it is *right* to do so. Kant describes this realm as a Kingdom of Ends, a place or way of 'seeing' which regards the world from the perspective of the end, not of the means, which is that of the realm of the phenomenon.

It is in this Kingdom of Ends that we can begin to trace the existence of the beings and the precepts of the noumenal realm. For instance, instead of regarding other human beings as empirical individuals, subject to the storm and stress of the phenomenal nexus of causality, we regard them as *persons* and make our judgments upon this noumenal basis. The attribution of personality to the other is to regard her as an end in herself, a noumenal being worthy of respect. Moreover, in addition to the population of this kingdom, there are also its laws and its practical precepts which form the rational basis for a moral state of affairs. For instance, there is rational faith in the existence of God, the immortality of the soul, and in freedom itself.

While none of these ideas can be proven to the satisfaction of theoretical or empirical reason (which are merely two sides of a coin), they do have practical value amidst the intentionality of moral reason in its command of obedience to the moral law. For Kant, this practical realm, as it is characterised by unconditional freedom, is the transcendental condition of, and thus has primacy over, the theoretical deployment of reason.

Indeed, blind to its own *topos* of emergence in the world, theoretical reason conflates its own self-examination and its phenomenal chain with the world itself, which for Kant is actually of a broader significance than the phenomenon. Without this authentic ground in freedom, theoretical reason would not have even emerged as a possibility of a free pursuit of knowledge in the first place. Theoretical reason threatens to be a knowledge which undermines its own possibility in its negation of freedom. It is thus in a state of contradiction (without, that is, Kant's limitation of theoretical reason). In this way, for Kant, as with Levinas, ethics, or true morality, and not ontology, is *first philosophy*.

As it is concerned with the ends and not the means of action, practical reason concerns intentions and the moral legitimacy of any factical maxim. In this way, practical reason will determine the moral character of an action, not on the basis of its effect or whether or not such an action is desirable, but more significantly from the standpoint of reason, with respect to the coherence of maxims which announce and characterise various actions. Kant conceives of this event of determination, almost metaphysically, as the direct determination of the *Wilkür*, or the individual will, by the *Wille*, the will as reason itself. Yet, this is not the subsumption of a particular existence under a universal concept, even if we can demonstrate that such an application to the manifold is *just*. On the contrary, for Kant, the determination of the *Wilkür* by the *Wille* is an event of the self-determination of the will amidst the unity of reason. It is in this way that the direct determination of the will by reason is not to be conceived as a dictatorial assertion against the individual will, since, as rational beings, this determination is performed by ourselves, upon ourselves. This self-determination is autonomy and is the positive sense of freedom in the world, of moral action which, unaffected by heteronomous forces, is expressed by self-given maxims.

Kant unfolds his positive doctrine of morality in his explication of the means by which we express and judge our maxims which pretend to moral legitimacy. The procedure by which he is able to judge the moral worth of a maxim is through a strategy of Universalisation. In his own words, a maxim is *just* if it can be willed as a 'universal law of nature'. For instance, my maxim may be that I should kill myself. Yet, examined in light of Kant's criteria, such a maxim, if universalised, would destroy humanity itself, and thus, would eliminate the *topos* for authentic freedom, autonomy and personhood. Thus, such a maxim is to be denied. An example which Kant gives is that of never lying. He believes that such a maxim could be universalised. Yet, there are many critiques of this famous example, such as 'What if a killer comes to the door and asks for a friend you know is hiding? Would it be just to lie?' Kant would seemingly answer that one must not lie. It is possible after all that the friend has jumped out of the back window and has fled. If I lie and say 'No!', the killer may walk around the house and see my friend fleeing.

Whether or not we can agree with Kant's judgment in this regard, a maxim which passes the test of universalisation becomes an imperative, a command of reason. Moreover, this imperative of reason, as practical, must have a place to be articulated, and, for Kant, this is that of autonomy. The latter is not however an autarky, but a rational *sensus communis* which determines not only the legitimacy of maxims, but also executes the determination of the will itself. This implication of a practical reason raises the question of the extent to which the *mores* of existing religious traditions determined Kant's moral sensibilities. There does seem to be a curtailment of individuality vis-à-vis his notion of autonomy. Yet, Kant is not unfolding an ethics of happiness, but of an absolutely necessary morality which would be at once social, as that of a community of rational beings. The highest maxim of this new morality, the Categorical Imperative, is irreducibly linked to social existence and to the other. One would imagine that such an imperative, having risen above any relative value or hypothetical imperative, would be that which is the most universal. It commands that the other is treated as an end, and never as a means *only*. I have emphasised this last word as it intimates a certain curtailment of universality in its seeming allowance of a loophole. Yet, Kant could easily answer that he is instead evoking the noumenal character of personhood, beyond the mere phenomenon as the realm of means.

Kant is not a Utopian Marxist or anarchist, as he believes that we will always be subjected to the horizons of possible experience, and thus, of the phenomenon as the realm of unfreedom, of deterministic causality, space and time. And, as there are many situations, some of which are quite imperfect, there will be some commands which are merely hypothetical and others which are indeed relative, and thus are not commands at all. It is, however, in our moral autonomy, in our noumenal selves, that we apprehend the universality and necessity of the moral law.

In this light, one could contend that there is a seemingly unbridgeable gulf between the theoretical and practical, necessity and freedom, and between each of these antitheses and the shape and flux of the lifeworld. We will examine Kant's negotiation of this divide, especially in the Transcendental Dialectic. Yet, it was the Third *Critique* which sought to bridge this gap and bring cohesion and unity to the Critical method.

Critique of Judgment (1790)

Following the Second *Critique* by two years, the Third *Critique* not only seeks to complete the Critical Philosophy on its own terms (though arguably not the *system* of transcendental philosophy), but also, to a marked extent, sets off in a new direction, one that was picked up by the German Idealists, Schopenhauer and others, and is the subject of questioning and debate to this day. The Third *Critique* seeks to bridge the gap between theoretical and practical reason through the bridge of aesthetic and teleological judgments. These judgments are facilitated by *concepts of reflection*, which are distinct in that they do not determine phenomenal objects, but consider them in a different light, in the free play between imagination and understanding. What Kant is suggesting is a different way to consider aesthetics – not as the space and time of theoretical reason, nor as the absence of the space and time from practical reason.

Instead, a non-theoretical aesthetics is set forth to allow for other facets of reason and existence to speak (such as art). In the first part on aesthetical judgment, we consider beauty and the sublime as another aspect or meaning/sense of the phenomenal world. This is not an indication, directly, of a noumenal domain, but, for Kant, is in between the phenomenon and noumena, strictly conceived. Aesthetics is a different way of looking at phenomena, which in the case of teleological judgment, may have an impact on the perspectives and methods of science itself as normally practised by theoretical reason. Indeed, as the middle, judgment in the sense of aesthetical and teleological reason allows us to begin to build a bridge between the disparities of reason. For instance, with the beautiful, Kant speaks of the phenomenon not in the sense of strict, necessary and universal knowledge, but in the sense of its affectation upon us. Beauty is the harmony of the imagination and understanding, and, Kant adds, is shared by all in the *sensus communis* which possesses similar capacities and sensibilities. In this example, beauty becomes an attribute of something in the phenomenal world, a way of speaking and fathoming the world, thereby including art (and imagination) upon the *topos* of reason. Such an inclusion also intimates, for Kant, the other realm of the noumena, as for instance, at the close of the 'Dialectic of Aesthetical Judgment', where he claims that the beautiful intimates the moral law itself and could be used to promote and facilitate public morality. Beauty then, as an aesthetic concept, would allow us to suspend the theoretical conditions of possible experience and work to re-define the meaning of the possible.

The next concept of reflection is that of the sublime, which is perhaps more significant as it contains within itself an explanation for the hegemony of transcendental subjectivity, of apperception, which becomes in the First *Critique*, the cornerstone of Kantian philosophy. The notion of the sublime – in the nineteenth century in the hands of artists, musicians and poets – has increasingly emerged since the twentieth century as a central aspect of a renewed reflection upon and expression of the relation of art and the sacred. The sublime, in its differing senses, that of the mathematical and dynamical, discloses that which is threatening to the mortal subject. However, unlike in the case of the beautiful, the faculties of imagination and understanding do not remain in harmony. Indeed, in this event, it seems that the two faculties vie, one with the other, in the pursuit of mastering the sublime phenomenon. The imagination seeks to imagine the phenomenon as a totality, to grasp it, while the understanding stands on waiting to see the results of this attempt. However, for Kant, the imagination fails to grasp the totality, and its failure is such that Kant's previous demotions of this faculty become increasingly clear. For, in the wake of the failure of imagination, it is understanding, and its ground of unity in reason, which is supreme, even in relation to the sublime, as it can conceive of this sublime object, however large or small, however chaotic and uncontrollable, as merely its own representation. It is merely an object for consciousness, and it is therefore nothing without this ground in the representational web of consciousness. The imagination (Art?) has failed and is thus merely put to work amid the designs of reason and understanding which set rational limits to its will.

Another concept of reflection, which is detailed in Part Two of the Third *Critique* is that of teleological judgment. As with the beautiful and sublime, teleological reason is another way to consider or to look at the phenomenal world. As we will see below in Kant's discussions of substance and the existence of God from the perspective of theoretical reason, questions of *teleology* must remain undecided. However, from the perspective of the faculty of reflective judgment, we may consider the exteriority of the causal nexus with respect to the intentionality of its development to an *end*, as with Aristotle's example of an acorn which becomes an oak tree. As we know, the latter's sense of *telos* is beyond the horizons of the possibility of experience. We cannot experience a *telos* in that its possibility speaks of an inside to the outside of the web of representations, similar to Schopenhauer's will. While Kant would not endorse the latter, he would suggest that amid our rational contemplation of nature, we find from the Third *Critique* an echo of the *regulative principles of reason*, in the Transcendental Dialectic, which demand that we construct various heuristic concepts which, while not theoretically determinant, have a regulative purpose in our understanding of the sense and direction of the whole.

Religion within the Limits of Reason Alone (1793)
Published three years after the Third *Critique*, *Religion* is not regarded in the same light as the three Critiques as it is mainly a polemical work on the meaning of true morality and thus of a *religion within the limits of reason*. What makes this work very valuable from a hermeneutical perspective, is Kant's unashamed presupposition of the Critical Philosophy. In this way, we almost uniquely witness the interaction and negotiations between the three typologies of reason in the context of the ethical question of the significance and practice of religion in relation to Kant's own Categorical Imperative. The work is, moreover, interesting in light of the fact that it was the first he published after being censored in a government crackdown on his religious views. In the Preface to *Religion* he basically acquiesces to the ban on his writings on the topic of religion, but only from standpoint of the public intellectual.

As a private individual, he could explore any topic he would deem reasonable. It may seem that such a strategy impinges upon his personal autonomy and the status of his moral judgment and courage. Yet, Kant makes it quite clear that this is only the strategy of a tightrope walker who is re-adjusting himself. For, throughout this text, he sets forth a ruthless and iconoclastic attack on traditional forms of religion, dogma, ritual, and even prayer. His basic position is that none of these are necessary, and that all one needs is respect for the moral law. He does concede, however, that not everyone is immediately capable of reaching the ideal and that such makeshift 'idols' would be necessary, as with art and nature, as intimations of the moral law. However, these remain 'idols' nevertheless, or, as Wittgenstein muses, ladders to be thrown down.

CHAPTER 2

OVERVIEW OF KEY THEMES

OVERVIEW

In this section, I shall outline the major themes that will emerge in our discussion of the *Critique of Pure Reason*. This overview of themes will serve as a preliminary introduction of topics which will be analysed in more detail in our actual reading of the text. This section will give the reader a *prospective* familiarity with the purpose, scope and composition of the *Critique of Reason*. We will consider the following themes:

A priori: The *a priori* is a central notion for Kant as it intimates true knowledge, which has the character of strictness, necessity and universality. The *a priori* is generally defined as that which is known without the aid of experience. Yet, it is the peculiar sense of the *a priori* as capable of *synthetic* employment that is indicated in Kant's question, 'How are synthetic *a priori* judgments possible?' The solution to this question would allow Kant not only to preserve the *a priori* against sceptical, empiricist attacks, but would also allow him to re-define the *a priori* in a way that differed from the merely analytic *a priori* of the rationalists.

A posteriori : The *a posteriori* is a notion that is inextricably linked to the *a priori*. Indeed, it is the latter's opposite, indicating a type of knowledge without necessity and universality and generated from the synthetic representations of experience. However, in light of Kant's overriding project, not all synthetic judgments are *a posteriori*, but only those which arise out of experience. This type of knowledge is the centrepiece to the empirical philosophies of Locke and Hume.

The Copernican Revolution: Kant used this metaphor for the practice of his own philosophy as a revolution in the meaning of *a priori* knowledge. He outline two scenarios for the possibility of *a priori* knowledge, either it comes from the object or from the subject. Against the empiricists, he stated that *a priori* knowledge could never come from the object, from experience, as this is characterised by receptivity, by the necessity of being effected by a contingent object. On the other hand, Kant declared that he could conceive of an *a priori* knowledge grounded in the subject, prior to experience. It is the task of his philosophy to show how this is possible.

Ideality of Space and Time: In the Transcendental Aesthetic, Kant lays out a doctrine of sensibility which is quite distinct from the doctrines of either the empiricists or the rationalists. In opposition to the contention that sensibility was characterised only by the receptivity of sensation upon a passive subject, Kant describes sensibility as the projection of an *a priori* pure intuition in the subject. This pure intuition is divided into the forms of intuition which actively form the structure of the empirical realm with respect to time and space. Pure intuition is also a formal intuition of space and time which can serve as an *a priori* manifold for the construction of *a priori* sciences such as mathematics. In this way, space and time are aspects of our active consciousness, and not either things in the world, or derived from the empirical order via inductive generalisation.

Transcendental Logic: The first part of the Transcendental Analytic (that inquiry, as distinct from the Transcendental Aesthetic, which concerns the pure concepts and principles of understanding and reason), transcendental logic is distinguished from a general or formal logic on the basis that the latter is not at all concerned with content, but only its three laws of identity, contradiction and the excluded middle. On the other hand, transcendental logic is a development of Leibniz's *Principle of Sufficient Reason* which contends that every conditioned object (or any object as such) must have a reason for its existence. In the context of the First *Critique*, transcendental logic is that logic which describes the conditions of the possibility of experience. It is thus a 'logic' which transcends to the world, making judgments in a synthetic and *a priori* manner.

Authority of Reason: The authority of reason became a central question and problem at the close of the eighteenth century as empiricists and rationalists engaged in a battle over the meaning of philosophical truth and the ultimate criteria of knowledge. A tyrannical image of reason was disseminated by the empiricists, while the rationalists advocated reason as a liberating and enlightening power of human knowledge. The conflict between the two sides came to a head in the 1780s in the 'Pantheism Controversy' which concerned the legitimacy of reason to have authority in knowledge. After some vacillation, Kant came down on the side of the rationalists, but with his own apology for the authority of reason.

Autonomy: As the notion implies etymologically, autonomy is a power to give a law, or *nomos*, to oneself. The notion plays a central role in Kant's Second *Critique* and is briefly introduced as the state of freedom in the practical employment of reason. It concerns both a positive and a negative freedom. The latter is the freedom from the influences of the sensible world in matters of moral judgment. In the former, it is the freedom to choose between differing choices in the moral realm. Overall, autonomy is an unconditioned freedom which lies outside of the series of empirical conditions.

The Meaning of a Critique of Pure Reason: A criticism of pure reason for Kant is the only way for metaphysics to be engendered in the form of a science. Over against the unbridled power of pure reason in rationalism, and taking heed of the sceptical criticisms of reason, Kant set forth a variant of reason, the ideas of which are merely regulative, and not constitutive of the world.

The Limits of Possible Experience: *Possible* experience is an experience which is not only logically possible, in that it does not violate the principle of contradiction, but it is also, and more importantly, capable of manifestation in the empirical domain within the horizons and limits of time, space and causality, et al. For instance, a politician who is honest may be a possible experience, but the idea of honesty, or of a perfect state, is not.

The Justice of Human Knowledge (Quid Juris): Transcendental Deduction: After Kant lays out the pure intuitions and the pure concepts of the understanding, he asks the question of the right of the concepts to be applied to experience. The possibility of this question lies in the fact that concepts do not arise out of experience, but are to be applied to the latter in an *a priori*, synthetic fashion. His answer is given in the Transcendental Deduction, but it is an answer which is far from completely clear in light of the revisions of this section between the first two editions of the *Critique of Pure Reason*. Yet, the basic result of the Deduction is that concepts have such a right in light of their role as conditions of the possibility of experience. Without concepts, there is no experience (since the latter is the synthetic combination of time, space and concepts). As the argument goes, in that there is experience, there must be concepts of the understanding.

The Status of Imagination: The question of the status of the imagination will rear its head throughout the First *Critique*. While the imagination performs all of the synthetic activities of consciousness, there is a question of its status as a faculty in its own right. Kant is inconsistent on this point, not only between the First and Second Editions, but also within each of the Editions themselves. It is a central question, one which still has no satisfactory solution.

Phenomena and Noumena: These notions indicate Kant's grand division of reality into the sensible and intelligible realms. The former concerns the domain of experience, and in this way is a synthesis of representations in the temporal, spatial and conceptual order. This is the domain of proper knowledge. The noumenon (*Ding an sich*), on the other hand, does not exist in the empirical realm of the phenomenon, but serves in the First *Critique* as its intelligible ground. It is not capable of being known however, but can only be thought. The noumenon will have broader significance in the Second *Critique* which concerns the moral and practical domain of rational faith.

Schematism: The schematism is an important section of the First *Critique* which attempts to demonstrate the precise operations of the application of concepts to the empirical realm. The schematism is necessary as pure concepts cannot be directly and synthetically applied, but require a 'third' which mediates between sensibility and the understanding. This 'third' is the imagination, and the question of its status is once again raised with respect to its indispensable role in the formation of knowledge. The mediation requires a schema for each concept, and the results of the synthesis of sense and concept are synthetic *a priori* judgments, or the Principles of Pure Reason.

The Principles of Pure Reason: The principles arise from the Schematism, or, in other words, from transcendental judgment. Each is, for Kant, an example of synthetic *a priori* knowledge, and in their four divisions or types, they describe the totality of possible experience. Each division or type corresponds to a division in the Table of Concepts, and thus concerns the application of the concepts, or categories, of Quantity, Quality, Relation and Modality to the domain of experience.

Transcendental Dialectic: This is the final part of the Transcendental Analytic and concerns the self-generated illusions of reason in its drive for absolute truth. These illusions or errors, arising not from sensation, but from judgment, are not simply rejected and eliminated, but are archived as features in the self-exposition of a reason that generates these errors by necessity. The Dialectic is divided into the Paralogisms, the Antinomies and the Ideal of Pure Reason, concerning psychology (the soul), cosmology (the world) and theology (God), respectively.

Unconditioned: The unconditioned is that state which is, as the word implies, free of conditions. To a significant extent, it is another name not only for the *a priori*, but also for the transcendental conditions (for the condition*ed*) that Kant spells out in the First *Critique*. A primary role for this notion is disclosed in the Transcendental Dialectic, in which, in several ways, reason insatiably seeks out the totality of the conditions for any given conditioned. As reason traces the conditions in more depth, and the conditions of these conditions, at the end, it comes (at least ideally) to that which transcends each and every condition. For Kant, this state is only an 'idea', but one that is necessary as a guide and standard for the employments of understanding in the empirical realm. Also, it acquires an important status in the practical realm as this latter is already grounded in autonomy and freedom as original varieties of the unconditioned.

The Regulative Employment of the Ideas of Pure Reason: The crucial result of the *Critique of Pure Reason* is that reason must be limited in its employment to the intelligible domain and must not transgress the horizons of possible experience. Indeed, such a transgression could only be an imposture as the Ideas of reason by necessity transcend the horizons of possible experience. However, the Ideas of reason must have a regulative role for knowledge, guiding the understanding to ever more remote conditions under the ideal of an absolute knowledge.

BACKGROUND OF THE TEXT

In the main body of the Reader's Guide, I will be referring to the Norman Kemp-Smith (NKS) translation of *Kritik der Reinen Vernunft*. The superiority of this translation lies in its unabridged presentation of the first (A) (1781) and second (B) (1787) editions of the *Critique of Pure Reason*. The difference between these editions, especially with respect to the character and role of the imagination, is submerged in the more recent editions which uncritically favour the Second Edition. These alterations are significant throughout the text, but especially in the Transcendental Deduction, the Principles of Pure Understanding and the Paralogisms of Pure Reason, in which Kant found it necessary to provide complete or at least major restatements of these sections.

In this way, not only will I set forth a sequential exposition of the First *Critique*, I will also examine the transformations between the editions and the philosophical and historical reasons for these alterations. Such an examination will shed additional light on the major themes and purposes of the text and will allow the reader to fathom the state of incompletion and place of contestation that is the unstable identity of the *Critique of Pure Reason*. It is insight into the imperfection of the text which will allow us to comprehend subsequent philosophers, the German Idealists, Schopenahuer and a host of others, who have sought to rectify, complete, and in some senses to overcome the philosophy of Kant. We will explore a sample of the variety of responses to and appropriations of Kant in the last chapter, *Reception and Influence*.

Introduction: Kant and Transcendental Idealism
The philosophical writings of Kant have had an undeniable and indelible impact on the history and method of philosophy. Indeed, this impact is significant to this very day, not only in the vast amount of research that continues to be undertaken on Kant's own writings,

but also in the enormous influence that he has had on the great majority of subsequent philosophy over the last two centuries. It is clear that besides Descartes, Kant is the most important philosopher in the post-Enlightenment era. In fact, one could argue that even in philosophical work which does not explicitly mention his name, his influence is at least implicitly *felt*, even if this influence is only present in either a silent acceptance or a rejection of his transcendental standpoints in theoretical philosophy, ethics, aesthetics or in his heuristic teleology of nature, so admired by Goethe.

It is also significant that one of the most daunting challenges in contemporary philosophy, that of the 'Analytic/Continental divide', hinges on his name. Indeed, it has been argued in many quarters, from both sides of this divide, that the basic attitude to the Kantian philosophy has determined to a great extent many of the current debates *in* philosophy and *between* philosophical standpoints of the current era.

Yet, before we delve more deeply into the impact of Kantian philosophy upon our own philosophical situation, it would be helpful to set out a basic understanding of the type of philosophy Kant elaborated, which is that of *transcendental idealism*. Moreover, while this philosophy will be articulated in great detail in the following pages, a general perspective on its basic orientation will allow the student to situate the Kantian philosophy amid the broad and diverse tendencies of post-Enlightenment philosophy on the Continent and in the Anglo-American tradition, both of which draw heavily on his writings. Such a basic orientation into his thinking will provide the student with an introductory schema of his thought and of some of its most important terminological expressions and nuances.

In the following introduction, therefore, I will set out such a basic orientation into his thinking which he articulated in his three critical works, the *Critique of Pure Reason* (the First *Critique*), *Critique of Practical Reason* (the Second *Critique*) and the *Critique of Judgment* (the Third *Critique*). For Kant, these works set out an exhaustive framework for the eventual propagation of a new system of philosophy, although he himself never claimed to have completed such a system.

The Philosophy of Kant: The Basics

While I will give a much more detailed account of the philosophy of Kant in later pages, and of the reasons for its emergence at the end of the eighteenth century, it is important for the student to have a basic grasp of his philosophy and of the context of its emergence. Indeed, a philosophy does not simply fall from the sky complete as in the allegedly revealed texts of the dominant religions. In fact, Kant worked out his Transcendental or Critical Philosophy over a period of three decades, with many false starts, revisions, transformations and moments of vision, which, one could argue, were influenced to a great extent by the exigencies of the prevailing political, cultural and historical climate of his philosophical and existential engagements. The *Critique of Pure Reason*, a treatise on the theoretical understanding, for instance, took over ten years to find its first definitive expression in 1781, one that was to be significantly (and, for Heidegger, tragically) altered six years later in its second edition in 1787.

Moreover, the effects of this particular instance of revision and transformation can be traced in the form and content of the Second *Critique*, the *Critique of Practical Reason*, dealing with morality, which appeared in 1786. The Third *Critique*, the *Critique of Judgment*, dealing with a philosophical aesthetics and teleology, published in 1792, again, was another instance of re-thinking and transformation, especially with respect to the status of the imagination and the introduction of a transcendental sense of *feeling*. It is in this way that the texts of philosophy differ from (most of) those of theology – each philosophical text emerges from the facticity and historicity of the philosopher, the latter being the major source of its articulation, and who is thus to be *held* responsible for its content. One may recall the example of Socrates who preferred to be executed for his teachings instead of blaming the 'foreign' gods *by means of which* he was alleged to have corrupted the young. It is the ethical autonomy, or indeed, the sovereignty, in Bataille's sense, of the philosopher that discloses the basic *topos* of freedom which is that of *critical* inquiry, this place of radical questioning – a search for truth which makes the philosopher, following Heidegger, 'guilty'.[4] And, it is Kant's *guilt*, his daring to raise questions in the face of traditional orthodoxy, which is the great merit of his philosophy and its continuing call to each human being to 'think for oneself', a call he articulated in his essential essay, 'What is Enlightenment?'

In light of this essay, it becomes immediately apparent that a merely historical approach to the philosophy of Kant would be insufficient, if not wholly misleading. To 'think for oneself' would be to raise oneself above these factical, empirical conditions to a transcendental, autonomous standpoint from which one can express the truth of existence within a situation in which the full ethical ramifications fall to the one who has taken the *step beyond* (*contra* Maurice Blanchot) into questioning. Such an insight is apparent from the opening pages of the First *Critique*, but it becomes increasingly clear in the subsequent *Critique* that it is amid the site of freedom that philosophy takes wing (Hegel), or emerges into the world. Indeed, the transcendental standpoint advocated by Kant does not in and of itself rely on historical (empirically conceived) conditions. In the Preface to the First Edition of the *Critique of Pure Reason*, he writes:

> Human reason has this peculiar fate that in one species of its knowledge it is burdened by questions which, as prescribed by the very nature of reason itself, it is not able to ignore, but which, as transcending all its powers, it is also not able to answer. (NKS, Avii)

This statement is significant in that Kant is indicating a situation in which human reason finds itself in a most *untimely* predicament. And, contrary to Nietzsche's contention that only a few tragic individuals are the conduits of truth/untruth, Kant is insisting that all humans, indeed, all rational creatures, are untimely to the extent that they participate in the *community* of reason. Yet, as creatures of fate, of those who are subject to the conditions of finitude, we are not merely rational, eternal beings, but ones who are embedded in a dark perplexity due to our situation of embodiment, of existence. We have intimations of the truth, we seem to possess it, though when we seek to grasp it, we once again find ourselves in a situation of doubt and conflict, of antinomy. There is a duality in our state of being – we are, with Aristotle, gods *and* animals. We find ourselves *in between* these two states of being, haunted by eternity *and* timeliness, between the grace of *pure reason* and the doom of *pure animality*.

In this way, our predicament may lead immediately, and drastically, to one of two destinations: *either* to the dogmatism and enthusiasm of *rationalism* or to the scepticism and barbarism of *empiricism*. Kant, like Odysseus, however, seeks to find a *middle course* between these Scylla and Charybdis. What Kant is saying in the preceding quotation is that our situation of perplexity in the face of two equally reprehensible options will not be abated by a decision in favour of one or the other option. Perplexity will always remain – that is endemic to our situation. Any decision causes to resurface the basic state of the original decision, much as Sisyphus who was condemned eternally to push a boulder up a mountain only to have it fall back down again when he seemed to have reached his goal. That is our empirical and real-politic predicament. However, for Kant, as free, autonomous beings, we can never be forced to choose between two (or more) illusory, and detrimental, options. As free, we may take a *step back* and *think for ourselves* in the wake of our situation of finite (forced) choice. And, more significantly, we can *choose not to choose*.

For Kant, there is yet another way to proceed, one that, as it may acknowledge each of these supposed positions, lays out a differing terrain by which we can come to terms with our situation of perplexity and attempt to construct a workable framework by which we can – at the same time – set out a *topos* of finite understanding with respect to knowledge, and a practical orientation in matters of our ethical existence. This *topos* is transcendental or critical philosophy, a place *between* and *beyond* the unsavoury options of rationalism and empiricism, of the either/or of enthusiasm and barbarity.

For Kant, the entire drama of reason and existence can be found in ourselves, in each one of us – indeed, in all rational beings, as I have suggested. We are all and each fated, as Caputo so elegantly writes, amid the 'dark night of existence'. The perplexity into which reason throws us, however, is not necessarily something we should mourn. Amidst the community of reason (of the *sensus communis* of Kant in the Third *Critique*), we can attempt to understand our situation and lay out its limits, to specify the various compartments of our apprehensions of the world – and the most appropriate *actions* for our most urgent tasks and aspirations. We must be able to *think for ourselves* in the wake of this perplexity. And, we can, as we divine one makeshift orientation after another.

One significant intimation of our autonomy, of this freedom from false, illusory choices, is Kant's announcement of his 'Copernican Revolution'. Engaging the question of how it would be possible to have philosophical truth, or *a priori* knowledge, Kant asks the further question of whether it would come from the object or the subject. If we were to accept that truth came from the object, we would be, for Kant, merely subject to the *a posterori* contingencies of empirical receptivity. We would be merely passive receivers of data and would be thrown into the maze of the *epistemological fallacy*. Truth can never come from the object (and we will see why this situation of *un-freedom* is impossible in the following pages). But, given that we seek *a priori* truth, Kant can, as he says in the Introduction to the *Critique of Pure Reason*, readily accept the possibility of such truth if we accept that the basis of this truth lies *somehow* in the subject, before 'experience'.

As anyone would know from the history books, Copernicus articulated a cosmological doctrine which displaced the *geo-centric* dogmas of the Roman Catholic Orthodoxy (and thus, the *deep* ideology [theology] of Christendom) with a radical theory of a *heliocentric* universe, a belief the adherence to which led many, such as Giordano Bruno, to be burned at the stake. Kant took this latter theory aboard as a metaphor in which the universe did not merely circle around us so that we would be merely passive receivers, but that we, as the sun, circle around all that exists. Contrary to the rationalists and the empiricists of the day, Kant posited an *active* consciousness that, in an *a priori* fashion, determines, in its own way, the being of all that exists, and from out of a web of heuristic, situational projections, it constructs the phenomenon, according to its own inherent capacities. The form of appearance is orchestrated by the pure intuitions of space and time, and by the concept, each of which is a capacity of our active consciousness. But, this is not a return to a rationalism of 'innate ideas' and to the placid eternity and grace of a 'rational' universe, dependent on the will of a creator. As free, rational *and* sensuous beings, we are still embedded in perplexity, even if we spin around the cosmos as the sun (or an earth which has been un-seated from its position of a stable eternity). Kant seeks to express our freedom, but also to disclose the specific character of this freedom, as absolute in its autonomy, but, at the same time, bound in its acts by the parameters of *possible experience*.

This latter phrase is an allusion to Kant's debt to Hume, who he said awoke him from his own 'dogmatic slumber' in a rationalism which had become a 'mere play amongst concepts'. The meaning of a *critique* of pure reason – the meaning of a transcendental philosophy as such – is thus a rejection of any doctrine which advocates an immediate apprehension of eternal truths *à la* rationalism or revelation. And, while Kant does not accept the barbarism of empiricism, he posits the necessity of the *conditions of possibility of experience* amidst which any legitimate philosophical activity can find determination and expression. Pure concepts will only play amongst themselves and will have no relation to the world, just as mere experience can never yield *a priori* truth. It is the *middle-world* which will disclose the possibility of a synthetic knowledge that is at once *a priori*, a knowledge which transcends the criticisms sustained by either pure concepts or pure experience.

For Kant, this middle course does indeed begin with the facticity of 'experience'. However, as he is seeking *a priori* truth, or that truth which possesses the character of strict necessity and universality, he takes a step back into the *transcendental* question. In the face of this experience, he asks after *the conditions of possibility* for this phenomenon or what makes this thing or state possible. His answer is that we can only know that which *we have placed there ourselves*, that there is, in other words, *something* about the transcendental subject that makes experience possible. This *something* is the *a priori* conditions of consciousness or mind which are projected from ourselves to construct and organise the manifold of experience. These *a priori* conditions, as we will examine in detail in the following pages, are the pure intuitions of time and space (*transcendental aesthetic*) and the pure concepts (*transcendental logic*). Each of these *a priori* conditions is seated in a faculty of the consciousness of the subject, the former in the faculty of *pure intuition*, the latter in the *pure understanding*. These conditions are *pure* in that knowledge arises at the instigation of experience, but not out of experience. Moreover, it is the *synthetic unity* of these conditions through the imagination, with its seat in the transcendental subject, which allows experience to become manifest as objects in the world. In this light, it is due to the *a priori* construction of experience that the objects we experience are not those of empiricism, but those of our own active consciousness.

Indeed, there is never simply a naïve object *there* for us. As objects of experience are always the result of the synthetic projections of the mind in time, space and causality (one of the twelve *pure concepts of the understanding*), we are always already ourselves *in the way* when we seek the thing-in-itself (*Ding an sich*). In fact, it would be wrong to state that there is an object there at all, like a table or a chair, that in the face of which we somehow stand (as if, with Leibniz, our cognition is somehow imperfect). For Kant, all objects of experience are constructions of our minds amidst a web of representational consciousness, and beyond this nexus of experience, he states, there is only an 'X'. This 'X' is the *transcendental object*, that upon which we project time, space and causality, et al., and, of which, we have no knowledge whatsoever. At the same time, our embedded-ness in our own field of representation does not mean that we are simply in a *solipsistic* state of irretrievable subjectivism, as the web of representations, the *conditioned*, is ultimately referred to the *condition* which is this transcendental object. The only proviso, however, is that we can never *theoretically* know this transcendental condition.

We will see, however, in the Second *Critique*, that we do have access to this transcendental condition in a practical, moral way. It is just not susceptible to *knowledge*, in the strict sense, but instead to what Kant entitles rational faith (and arguably to the state of aesthetic contemplation as set forth in the Third *Critique*). It is in this way that Kant sets out a strict meaning for the term *knowledge* and this meaning is limited to the field of representation alone. Much of what is 'new' in Kant circles around this strict definition of knowledge. This will become more clear as we delve more deeply into the Kantian philosophy.

It is his new 'model of the mind',[5] that of an active, synthetic consciousness, which departs from both rationalism and empiricism. And, as we will see in more detail below, this is not a mere presupposition that is asserted by Kant, but is the necessary result of our own situation of practical freedom and autonomy – of the active life of reason. Of course, as Kant will readily admit, most of the time, we as empirical subjects behave in a way similar to that described by Hume. However, in that we are seeking *a priori* truth amidst the facticity of existence, there must also be the recognition that we are more than the one-dimensional men (Marcuse) of the empiricists. Our transcendental character is not merely an assumption, a *deus ex machina*, which provides a means of escape, but is a necessary dimension of our existence as free, autonomous beings. In this way, for Kant, we are 'double-headed', creatures of sensibility and intelligibility, but in such a state of being that the transcendental dimension of our character has priority as it alone can account not only for our capacity of *a priori* knowledge but also for our state of practical or moral freedom. It is this priority which discloses the character of *transcendental* philosophy.

The Topos of Departure: Beyond Rationalism and Empiricism

In the introduction above, I indicated that Kant's Critical or Transcendental philosophy emerged as a response to a dire conflict between rationalism and empiricism at the end of the eighteenth century. This was a complex and serious controversy which involved the most important names in the philosophy of the time. And, to make such a characterisation of a philosophical era even more complicated, there were extremely unlikely bed-fellows on each side of this divide, a divide which was probably more serious than the current divide between Analytic and Continental philosophy. On the one hand, there were the rationalists such as Mendelssohn and Wolff who set out from the philosophies of Descartes, Spinoza and especially Leibniz. Indeed, for those in the know such a concatenation of names in itself may provoke astonishment in light of the massive controversies between each of these grounding philosophers in their own era. On the other hand, there were the empiricists Jacobi and Hamann, the Romantics, such as Schiller and Goethe, and the radical atheist Hume. This grouping will also provoke an equal astonishment as such a range of thinkers included the most pious of religious thinkers such as Jacobi and the most atheistic such as Hume. Yet, what stood at the heart of the controversy were the questions of the *authority of reason* and of its proper limits. This entire battle is detailed admirably by Friedrich Beiser in his authoritative work, *The Fate of Reason*. Suffice it to say for now, that the dispute between the rationalists and the empiricists struck at the heart of the question of the very meaning of philosophy itself, and as I have suggested, this question circled around the question of the authority of reason.

Thinkers such as Jacobi were cast into near panic by the pretensions of reason to *enlighten* the world as expressed in the philosophies of Spinoza and Leibniz. Although these two thinkers differed radically, that which they shared was the presumption that reason itself was the ground of all thought and being – Spinoza envisioned a progressive destruction of superstition and religiosity with the growing enlightenment of reason, while Leibniz stated that even God must conform to the laws of reason. Jacobi et al. saw this as an atheistic or at least as a 'pantheistic' subversion of the immediate truths of revelation and faith which for him were empirically grounded. It is of course ironic that Hume, a devout atheist, set forth an interpretation of empiricism which in no way was consistent with that of Jacobi. But, both remained sceptical of the truths of reason and in this strange way were allies in this controversy. In the following pages,

I would like to analyse the differences between rationalism and empiricism through an exploration of two of the most emblematic proponents of this divide, Leibniz, for the rationalist camp, and Hume, for the empiricists. It will be from this analysis that we will be able to comprehend the emergence of the Kantian *middle course* of transcendental philosophy, one which was both a synthesis and a displacement of this controversy. Indeed, with Kant this controversy seemed to end almost immediately to the disdain of both sides. It is to the credit of Beiser that we remember the historical *topos* of the emergence of Kantianism at all, for most of his predecessors have fallen away into near oblivion. But, anticipating remarks I will make at the close of this Reader's Guide, it seems to have become necessary to re-examine this dispute due to the increasing uncertainty that has arisen, especially in the context of contemporary Continental philosophy, over the apparent success of Kant's silencing of it. This is apparent also in the continuing battles characteristic of the Analytic/Continental divide which stem from the uneasy synthesis of empiricism and rationalism in the Kantian philosophy.

Leibniz

I have chosen Leibniz to represent the rationalists, for while he lived and worked in the seventeenth century, his philosophy was the most dominant influence on the rationalists, Wolff and Mendelssohn, who were each the immediate source of the philosophical instruction of Kant. And, though a rationalist, Leibniz served to a great extent as a model for a philosophy which sought to curtail the most unashamed rationalist excesses of philosophies of the type of Spinoza. Indeed, the bad word in the eighteenth-century dispute, from the side of the empiricists, especially of Jacobi, was the charge of 'Spinozism!' (e.g. against Lessing, not to mention the later 'atheism' controversy between Jacobi and Fichte). Leibniz, although he maintained an ultimately rationalist position, at least attempted to maintain that the factical world had necessary significance and would not be swallowed by an ever more voracious reason.

In the following, I will lay out a brief portrayal of the philosophy of Leibniz as set forth in his works, the *Monadology* and the *Discourse on Metaphysics*, in light of its significance for the interpretation of Kant that is to follow.[6]

The term rationalism derives from the Greek *ratio* which means 'cut', but it has also been deployed as a synonym for the term *logos*, which while beginning as a word to describe 'voice', began to signify with Heraclitus and the other Pre-Socratic philosophers, such as Parmenides, the intelligible structure of being and of thought. Yet, the significance of the metaphor of cutting or severing increasingly gained the upper hand in philosophy, especially after Xenophanes and Parmenides, in the radical distinction between the sensible and the intelligible realms of being and thought. This cutting gained its classic formulation in the philosophy of Plato with his 'divided line'. In this way, Leibniz divided the entirety of the world into two realms, that of *truths of fact* and *truths of reason*.

Beginning with the realm of facticity and contingency, the truths of fact are those of the everyday situations and events which confront us in the domain of finite existence. These facts are not accessible to certainty and clarity in the manner of Descartes since, as Husserl describes in his *Phenomenology of Internal Time-Consciousness*, they could be otherwise. This is the synthetic, *makeshift* existence in which we are embedded, where things are posited together, joined, mixed, changeable, mutating. There is neither necessity nor certainty in this realm, and the search for necessary truth, which is the task of the philosopher, would ultimately prove itself to be futile. All that is possible in this realm, at least for the mortal being, with respect to the question of truth, is *inductive generalisation*, which as we will see is the only recourse in the philosophy of Hume. We can only attempt to make generalisations from our experience and state these results in propositions of a *synthetic* character.

For instance, we can say 'the ball is red', but the truth of our statement can only be verified by experience, by experiment, in which we test this statement of fact. The predicate 'red' is not included in the definition of the subject 'ball', as balls can be other colours. In the synthetic realm, we are always subject to the condition of receptivity and conditioned-ness and can never know anything *a priori*. All that is solid melts into air as we wait eternally for verification. But if I said 'the ball is round', I would not need to look to experience, as round is included in the definition of the subject. This would be an analytic proposition, one which gives rise to necessary, though merely tautological, truth. In this light, for Leibniz, the synthetic realm is not the only place to look for the philosopher in his or her search for truth.

For Leibniz, *beyond* and *before* the truths of fact are the truths of reason. These are the *thoughts of God before creation* and to which, for Leibniz, the finite creature can aspire for attainment. From out of the abyss of temporality and utter contingency, Leibniz indicates that we are also conscious of eternal truths, those of logic and mathematics, which intimate our participation in a realm of truth which transcends our condition of finite facticity. For *some reason*, we are cognisant of the truths of logic, as articulated by Aristotle, of the principles of identity, of contradiction, and of the excluded middle. And, we have access to the truths of mathematics, which were very close to Leibniz's own heart as he, independently of Newton, discovered the mathematics of calculus. Indeed, we still use his notions to this day in *differential* calculus, having long ago forgotten the *fluxions* of Newton. However, this realm of eternal truth is not merely a *beyond* to which we may hope to escape, but it is indeed a *before* as a *condition of possibility* for this contingent realm of facticity itself.

It is in this way that Leibniz discloses to us another eternal truth which is detected in our consciousness, and a fourth, and indeed, for him, *the* grounding law of logic in *the principle of sufficient reason*. This principle, the forerunner for Kant's transcendental logic and aesthetic as conditions of possibility, states simply that any being or thought has a reason or ground for its existence. Such a reason or ground, for Leibniz, is an eternal truth, and exists in the 'mind of God' as the sufficient reason for the ephemeral, synthetic, truth of finite contingency.

Yet, as I have suggested, these realms are not *ultimately* distinct. For, from the 'perspective' of God, the reason for each contingent fact would be disclosed, as He can instantaneously plumb the depths of contingency. Each mortal fact has its own reason, or in other words, each synthetic truth can be reduced to that of the analytic. In this light, for Leibniz, the divine underpins all being, and all things, as with Berkeley, exist in a world which is the artwork of the divine. Even the subject of this mortal striving for truth is conceived as a substance, as a monad, who seeks perfection from out of its situation of mortal imperfection. The drive for perfection is rooted in its being as an *entelechy*, an appropriation of Aristotle, which indicates a striving for a certain perfection, for self-actualisation. The situation of this self-actualisation is the rational universe, conceived as a hierarchy of monads between the bare monad of the stone and of the soul in death, then of plants, animals and finally, the actualised monad in the living, rational being. Each of these monads, moreover, exists amidst the 'best of all possible worlds' in a *pre-established harmony*, one which is, however, dynamic, in the sense that each monad not only expresses in itself the truth of existence as the mirror of all being, but also as that which may be recalled into existence, to be re-awakened after any particular death so as to maintain this harmony (which, contrary to the Platonic notion of *metempsychosis*, is entitled *metaschematism*). Death in this way would not be conceived as a separation of a soul from a body, but only as a diminishment of body, and an envelopment back into the bare monad, into a sleep in the City of God, one that is to await another awakened state.

For Leibniz, the monad is self-contained, *windowless* in his metaphor, and thus seeks perfection, as an *entelechy*, in the confines and root of its own self. Kant will take issue with this substantialist conception of the subject which does not give any heed to the horizons of possible experience. While Kant will appropriate the striving self as the prototype for his own philosophy of an active consciousness, it is this *windowless* character which will provoke his charge that rationalism remains an analytical play amongst concepts. Kant will seek to take this striving monad to the world, as another meaning of *transcendental* philosophy, and in this way, the contribution of Hume cannot be underestimated. For Kant, truth cannot be merely analytic, but must be synthetic in an *a priori* sense. Such a goal however entails that we now turn to the dismissal of rationalism by the radical empiricist Hume. It is in Kant's appropriation and ultimate rejection of Hume that the lines of transcendental philosophy are more clearly drawn.

Hume

One of the most repeated anecdotes in the articulation of Kantian philosophy is that he was awoken from his dogmatic slumber by the philosophy of Hume. While there are always many 'takes' on what such a statement and admission may mean, what is significant is that in the first instance such an influence indicates that at the latter days of the eighteenth century there was an active inter-change of ideas across the Continent, so much so that the 29-year-old Hume, from Scotland, would have been read by Kant, who, approaching fifty, took notice of the *Treatise On Human Nature* (written when Kant was around 16) to such an extent that it changed his entire orientation towards philosophy as such. In the following section, I will outline the philosophy of Hume and attempt to disclose why his philosophy had such a dramatic impact on a middle-aged German philosopher who was already established in his own right. Hume, when he had the time to write philosophy amidst his many backgammon and drinking sessions, set out a philosophy which had such a dramatic and revolutionary impact that his writings to this day remain utterly fresh and continue to dominate many areas of philosophy.

The most dominant influence of Hume is his impact on rationalism and on the very possibility of *a priori* ideas. His influence is also virulent with respect to any attempt to establish *any* belief in a God. Indeed, from what we have already set forth with respect to the philosophy of Leibniz, we could state at the outset that his philosophy remains entirely within the realm of the truths of fact. I have already said that he was an untimely bedfellow of Jacobi et al., in questioning the authority of reason. His philosophy indeed is a radical questioning of the principle of sufficient reason and of any rationalist attempt to establish philosophical truth from the perspective of a mere idea.

In his *Enquiry Concerning Human Understanding*, Hume begins with the impressions of the senses as the immediate source of any possible source of truth. And, writing before Kant's First *Critique*, he had as his target the rationalist attempt to establish the *a priori* truth of reason. Indeed, it is not even clear if he would have accepted Kant's intervention and attempt to synthesise and displace the positions of rationalism and empiricism. With his beginning in the impressions of the senses, Hume states that any knowledge that we could ever have is based on the habitual association of certain impressions, gathered amid a process of inductive generalisation. In this way, we could compare his way of philosophy to the captives in Plato's cave who, still tied and captivated by the images and shadows on the wall, seek to associate the various images and shadows together into some kind of coherent pattern. As we sit chained to our seats, we seek to derive inductive associations and affinities amidst the myriad impressions which we receive. In our situation of receptivity, we have no hope of any *a priori* knowledge, and not even any immediate hope or prospect that we could ever be liberated from our servitude so that we could find our way out of the cave. In this way, all knowledge begins with the senses and stays with the senses. We, however, become acclimatised to our servitude and receptivity in the cave and become quite adept in our ability to trace out the associations and connections of the shadows on the wall. Through the habit of continued searching amidst the shadows on the wall we begin to gather through inductive generalisations certain habitual ideas about that which is being shown to us – our habits themselves become our ideas. Yet, even here it could be stated that amidst the slavish receptivity of captives in the cave an active consciousness is apparent, and surely Kant would have seen this.

In summary, for Hume, knowledge is built up from impressions and the habitual associations and affinities of these impressions in inductive generalisations into what we may wish to call ideas. For instance, the sun rises day after day, and we may wish to assert that the sun will rise again tomorrow. But, as we are slaves of the cave, we can never be ultimately certain of this fact as it has not yet occurred. We are creatures of impressions, habits and the ideas that are drawn from this basic state of facticity. Yet, as we become so accustomed to this condition of being and as there is no radical breach in this basic state, we are able to build and build upon our basic generalisation from impressions, and our ideas, although mere habits, take on a more permanent status. Hume seeks to critique not only rationalists such as Leibniz and his followers but also those pseudo-empiricists, such as Locke who set out his doctrine of primary and secondary qualities. For Hume, that which is primary must always be that of impressions derived from sensation. The primary qualities of Locke are indeed secondary, as are all ideas. The habitual associations become ideas, just as with the early Nietzsche's dictum that concepts are worn-out metaphors. The ultimate inference is that of God which is the ultimate idea, indeed the most extravagant inference from the habitual situation of impressive influence, and thus, that which is the most divorced from the primary sense data of impression. Indeed, in this way, all knowledge must always answer to the truth of the radical impressional facticity which is that of the receptive situation from which we can never escape.

Kant's Middle Course: Synthetic A priori Judgments

Kant immediately sensed the destructive potential of Humean empiricism, but instead of embracing an unabashed empiricism, which many of his friends such as Jacobi and Hamann saw as a potential in the Kantian philosophy, he sought to rescue the *a priori* and the authority of reason. However, his solution to this problem, though it did fall to the side of reason, gave enough ground to Hume that strict rationalists such as Mendelssohn contended that Kant had 'destroyed everything'. In the following, I will show how Kant developed his notion of synthetic *a priori* judgments through a criticism of both rationalism and empiricism and came up with an uneasy compromise that has to a great extent held up to this very day.

On the one hand, with Hume percolating in the background, Kant begins with a criticism of rationalism. He contends that rationalism, especially in metaphysics, would never be able to make any definitive claims about the world, such as those of physics and mathematics, and would always be susceptible to the radical scepticism of empirical philosophies such as Hume's. Rationalism is a 'mere play amongst concepts', and its analytic criterion of truth, which is signified most dramatically in the tautology of the first law of logic, can never achieve definitive verification in the world of experience. Indeed, as we will see in the Antinomies of the *Critique of Pure Reason*, from the rationalist standpoint, depending on our starting point, we may construct completely contradictory results deploying the same methods and rules of thought. All that a rationalist philosophy may give us, therefore, is a system of concepts, which while it may be internally consistent, will not have either any definitive protection against the antinomies of reason, nor be able to demonstrate any concrete relationship to the world of empirical facticity. As we have already seen, such a philosophy is rejected outright by Hume who stated that any system of concepts is merely a secondary array of *a posteriori* insights which can have no projective or predictive capacity with respect to the concrete world of experience. Yet, at the same time, Kant still sought to defend that which he saw as the core truth of rationalism, that of *a priori* knowledge and the *authority* of reason. He undertook to rescue the *a priori* through a transcendental criticism of Humean empiricism.

Kant sets out his criticism of Humean empiricism with the insight, as we have seen above, that while all knowledge begins with the empirical fact, it does not therefore arise out of experience. There exist *a priori* sciences such as mathematics and physics which may state the truth of experience even before experience is given to us as a manifold of representations. Kant argues that in these sciences there is the possibility of apodeictic certainty which is not susceptible to empirical scepticism (such as that of the Classical Syllogism, i.e. Major Premise: All men are mortal; Minor Premise: Socrates is a man; Conclusion: Therefore, Socrates is mortal). The method by which Kant establishes the possibility, indeed, this necessity, of apodeictic, synthetic truth, is that of *transcendental criticism*. To a significant extent, to which I have alluded above, this is a radical criticism of the Humean starting point in the mere impressions of the senses. Kant's primary example in this criticism is the notion of causality.

While Hume, from his own empiricist starting point sought to undermine the necessity inherent in any notion of causality, Kant contends that this notion, like each of the twelve pure concepts of the understanding (cf. below), has an *a priori* character. As I have suggested earlier, Kant holds that while knowledge is occasioned by experience, it does not arise out of experience. Knowledge, especially that with an *a priori* character, is that which is before experience, but as synthetic, has the capacity to be applied directly to experience. In the case of causality, this notion is not derived from the facticity of experience through habitual association and inductive generalisation, but is an *a priori* concept of an active consciousness which is projected upon the transcendental object in such a way that the very event of experience arises in the consciousness of the subject for the very first time. Since, for Kant, human knowledge is the irruption of the awareness of a free being (as we will see more clearly with a consideration of the Second *Critique*), this projection occurs prior to, or perhaps simultaneously with, the emergence of experience, this projection being the very construction of experience as a nexus of representations *there* as an object for consciousness. In this way, the active consciousness of Kantian transcendental philosophy displaces any merely *receptive* characterisation of its theoretical activity to the extent that it is an *anticipatory* consciousness – and this perhaps is the best characterisation of the meaning of the *a priori* in knowledge.

In this light, Kant is waging a philosophical battle on two fronts, but instead of merely seeking to destroy his opponents, he also seeks to learn and appropriate from each of them. On the one hand, with the rationalists, Kant is seeking to preserve the integrity of the *a priori* and of the principle of sufficient reason – but not as a mere play amongst concepts. On the other hand, with the empiricists, Kant is seeking to allow for the necessity of an empirical element in knowledge which in no way is simply sequestered as a secondary realm of the truths of fact. For the main criticism of the rationalists is the inapplicability of the truths of reason to that domain of fact with any certainty, or, in other words, the inability to have synthetic truth with an *a priori* character. It is in this way that Kant contends that all philosophical activity, as I have suggested above, must occur within the conditions of possibility of experience, which indeed, will have radical consequences, especially in any attempt to prove the existence of God. And, the main criticism of the empiricists is indeed the same, that they too disallow the possibility of *a priori* knowledge in the synthetic realm. It is in this way that Kant's notion of synthetic *a priori* judgments transcends both of these positions. This is the dual task of a *critique of pure reason* and simultaneously that of a *critique of pure empiricism*. For Kant, the character of knowledge can be neither that of the pure spontaneity of concepts which seek to, with the rationalists, intellectualise the world of experience, nor the mere receptivity of intuitions which, with the empiricists, seek to undermine any possibility of the *a priori*, and therefore, of certain truth in the sciences and of knowledge generally.

The middle course, as Heidegger describes in his *Kant and the Problem of Metaphysics*, is a characterisation of knowledge which is simultaneously that of receptive-spontaneity and spontaneous-receptivity. Both of these elements of human consciousness are necessary for authentic knowledge: intuition and concept, sensation and understanding. It is the union of these capacities in the transcendental subject which makes synthetic *a priori* knowledge possible. That which Kant is describing therefore is rational knowledge that seeks to step or transcend into the world, but one that respects the horizonal limits of the world, a philosophy, as we will see, which seeks, contrary to the likes of Spinoza, to limit knowledge to allow room for 'faith'. It is in this way that Kant put an end to, or at least postponed indefinitely, the controversy between the rationalists and the empiricists.

As we now turn to an actual reading of the First *Critique*, we should keep in mind the question of how such a synthetic *a priori* truth is possible (and indeed necessary), *how* it is grounded, along the pathway of theoretical reason. Our first task is to describe the theoretical determination of the phenomenal world from the standpoint of strict, necessary and universal knowledge. It is the representational nature of consciousness which will allow us to understand the utter complexity of the seemingly simple and naïve object that stands before us. If it were merely such a simple and naïve thing that oppresses us (and even controls our ideas), we would be forced to accept the position of Hume.

But, as we will see, this phenomenon is indeed very complex and determined by the aspects of aesthetic intuition, or sensation, and by logic (formally and transcendentally conceived) or conceptuality. These two stems of the tree of knowledge, when united, give forth the fruit of synthetic *a priori* knowledge will set the standard for the criticism of any claims to knowledge of a synthetic character outside the horizons of possible experience.

CHAPTER 3

READING THE TEXT

INTRODUCTION

Kant begins his analysis of human reason with the contention that metaphysics, the so-called 'Queen of the Sciences', has never been able to make a single inch of progress as it has always been mired in its own self-generated battles. Of course, he is criticising the rationalist metaphysics of nearly two millennia which he characterises as a mere play amongst concepts. His basic contention, as I have suggested above, is that apparently contradictory results seem to arise from a faculty which is supposed to have the fundamental character of 'unity'. Moreover, he contends that this battle *back and forth* between seemingly irreconcilable rationalist positions has given ground to the most radical and destructive scepticism in the hands of the empiricists and sceptics, who have, since the first millennium BCE, had little time for rationalism and its attempts to intellectualise the world. In this light, Kant, through his *Critique of Pure Reason*, is seeking to place metaphysics, indeed philosophy and knowledge itself, upon a new foundation which will not be susceptible to the attacks of scepticism. Ironically, as I have suggested above, it is from the incitement of one such radical empiricist, Hume, that he takes his point of departure, but in a way which would not have been at all amenable, as far as we can tell, to this noted Scotsman. With his contention that there exist synthetic *a priori* truths, Kant at once displaces the *interiorising* tendency of the rationalists and the *exteriorising* dispersion of the empiricists. In other words, there is an *a priori* knowledge that is applicable, and is able to transcend, out of the window, as it were, to the world. It will be the task of the *Critique of Pure Reason* to disclose the transcendental conditions of possibility which, existing in the very immediacy of human consciousness, make such a new founding of metaphysics possible. Much of course will be lost in this way, to the disdain of rationalists such as Mendelssohn. But, for Kant, such *sacrifices* will be necessary if we are not merely to throw the 'baby out with the bath water'. For, at the end of the day, that which is essential is *a priori* truth, or, in other words, necessity and universality in the sciences, such as mathematics and physics (which for Kant, are examples of sciences with the character of *a priori* truth), and in the most necessary science (*Wissenschaften*), metaphysics. For Kant, without such an *a priori* standpoint, all progress, and indeed, relevance of the sciences would be lost. However, he sets out a ray of hope from the start by stating that even if all knowledge and philosophy were to be engulfed in an all-encompassing barbarism, metaphysics would still remain untouched as the root of human existence.

As I stated earlier, the standpoint from which Kant sets out is his declaration of a 'Copernican Revolution' in philosophy. It is this declaration which sets out the character and the trajectory of the ground for the new metaphysics. As an obvious dismissal of the factical receptivity emphasised by Hume, Kant states that it is from the subject and not from the object that we possess our only capacity for *a priori* truth. For if we exist merely in the receptive posture vis-à-vis the objects of experience, empirically conceived, then there can only be *a posteriori* truth. However, from the standpoint of Kant's contention that the transcendental subject not only *is* free, but also *ought* to be free, both from the impressions of the senses and from the dogmatic servitude to the *mere* concept, a beginning in the *concrete* subject will allow for an *a priori* conceptualisation of the truth of the world. We have already had an indication of how such a synthetically *a priori* truth is possible amidst human existence. As I have stated, it is from a self-analysis of the subject that we will disclose the conditions of possibility for an *a priori* truth which is able to transcend into the world, being occasioned from the stimulus of the domain of experience, but not arising out of experience.

TRANSCENDENTAL AESTHETIC: SPACE AND TIME
(NKS 63; A17/B31)

As I have suggested, Kant sought to move beyond the entrenched positions of rationalism and empiricism by demonstrating that which both of these positions held to be impossible: synthetic *a priori* knowledge. This is quite clear with respect to Hume, as we have seen in his treatment of causality. It is a bit more difficult in the context of Leibniz as it could be argued that even a truth of fact has a sufficient reason. Yet, such a reason, for Leibniz, is still analytic, as he suggests that the realm of contingency is perfectly analysable into analytic truth, but only for an infinite mind such as that possessed by God. This is not possible for finite beings who are constrained within the horizons of temporality, and while we have examples of analytic truth in the tautology, we have our best hope of strict, necessary and universal truth in synthetic *a priori* truth. It will be the task of the following to show how such a truth is possible. This will necessitate the unfolding of the nexus of representational consciousness by means of a deconstruction of its elements, of sensibility and understanding, and of that which unites these stems of knowledge. That which will be revealed is the complexity of the realm of the phenomenon which is the object of our representational consciousness. In this section, I will examine the first stem of synthetic *a priori* knowledge with a consideration of sensibility which Kant presented in the Transcendental Aesthetic.

The Transcendental Aesthetic comprises what Kant entitles the pure forms of intuition, space and time. As we are not dealing with a Humean situation of empiricism, we immediately detect something quite different in Kant's treatment of sensibility. These forms of pure intuition are structures of consciousness projected upon the unknowable transcendental 'X' with the result that conditions of spatiality and temporality are generated in the manifold of experience. I will deal with each of these forms in turn, bringing them together at the end of the exposition with a consideration of the ground of possibility for an *a priori* space-time continuum and an *a priori* comprehension of the concept of causality.

On the one hand, there is the first pure form of intuition which is that of space. Kant designates our intuition of space 'outer sense', and it is the realm of the co-existence of all that is 'outside' of us. Everything in space is simultaneous in the room (*Raum*) that is projected by consciousness. Moreover, for Kant, in addition to being a pure form of intuition, space is also a pure formal intuition. In this way, within the very activity of our consciousness, there is an *a priori* intuition of space. Moreover, all spaces conceived in the plural are limitations of this *a priori* formal intuition of space. As an example of the significance of this notion, Kant declares that our entire ability to have an axiomatic, *a priori* geometry is made possible by this pure intuition of space. In this light, one of the first answers to our question, 'How are synthetic *a priori* judgments possible?' has been given in the transcendental condition of possibility of a pure apprehension of spatiality. Indeed, for Kant, such an apprehension does not rely upon any empirical experience of space. In fact, as the transcendental method of argument is set forth, any empirical apprehension of space always already relies upon this *a priori* capacity within our consciousness of reckoning with space as a pure form of intuition and as a pure formal intuition.

On the other hand, the second pure form of intuition that abides in our active, projecting consciousness is that of time. Time, which Kant entitles 'inner sense' is characterised by the pure form of succession. This succession for Kant as a pure form of intuition is disclosed as the formal organisation of our changing states, moods, thoughts, and of representations generally. Moreover, as with space, time is also immediately apprehended in our consciousness as a pure formal intuition, and therefore, all times are limitations of this one *a priori* time. And, as with space, all apprehensions of time in the empirical realm are grounded always already upon this pure formal intuition of time. We will see below that time itself is the primal form of consciousness.

In this way, for Kant, there is but a single space and a single time and both of these in their most fundamental character are *a priori* forms of intuitions and formal intuitions. These pure intuitions are discoverable within our own consciousness in an *a priori* manner, as disclosed through transcendental arguments, and there is thus no need to consult the empirical realm either to comprehend these intuitions or to construct these forms from some means of inductive generalisation from experience (as was the case with both Hume and Leibniz). Moreover, the unity of inner and outer sense constitutes the formal structure and *a priori* content (as pure formal intuitions) of the entire realm of pure sensibility. Yet, Kant will argue, in a way which would have a significant impact on the early Heidegger, that time has precedence over space as it is the most immediate formal structure of our subjective representations. Space, as outer sense, is only a mediate form of our pure sensibility and is determined in the last extent by the pure form of time. Moreover, for Kant, the unity of space and time in the space-time continuum is that which accounts for the *a priori* significance of the concept of causality. The notion that one state follows upon another with necessity relies upon the conditions of possibility of space and time for its intelligibility. That we can comprehend this concept in a purely *a priori* manner discloses the fact that causality is not to be derived, in the manner of Hume, from the empirical realm of experience, but is a concept which can be applied in an *a priori* manner to an *a priori* sensibility. And, as the pure intuition of space allowed us to comprehend the *a priori* character of geometry, the unity of space and time allows us to comprehend the *a priori* aspects of notions not only of theoretical physics, but also of any science that relies on the notion of causality.

The synthetic unity, or the *syndosis*, of space and time, moreover, is grounded for Kant in the transcendental imagination which is the ground of all synthesis. This will have a significant impact on the character of Kantian philosophy, and we will revisit this question throughout the following Reader's Guide, especially in the treatment given to the imagination in the Transcendental Deduction in the First Edition of the *Critique of Pure Reason* (the 'A' Deduction). Suffice it to say for now that this notion of an *a priori* imagination, and not merely the reproductive imagination of the empirical realm, will not only have a significant role to play in the entirety of the Kantian philosophy (even with its curtailment in the Second Edition of the First *Critique*, its apparent exclusion from the Second *Critique* and its quasi-restoration in the Third *Critique*), but, more significantly, as the archetype for the doctrine of *intellectual intuition* in the German Idealists Fichte, Schelling and Hegel. It is the imagination, as the faculty of synthesis, which is certainly one of the true answers to our question of the possibility of synthetic *a priori* knowledge, since, as the power of synthesis, it is able to bring together the manifold of experience in a way which does not rely on the presence of the empirical object. Indeed, Kant himself characterises the imagination as that which can *make present that which is not there*, in this case referring to the transcendental conditions of possibility, which, though not being there as objects, make experience possible in the first instance. Of course, Kant will have his own doubts about a *pure* power of the imagination (substituting for it in all but its title the power of combination of the understanding in the Second Edition [B, 1787] of the First Critique, in the *Transcendental Deduction*, cf. below), but the main argument still maintains its force, which is to disclose the possibility of synthetic *a priori* knowledge through a power of combination or synthesis which is not dependent upon the factical objects of the empirical realm.

Study questions

1. How does Kant justify his treatment of time and space as pure intuitions and not as pure concepts? How is this treatment related to Kant's criticisms of both empiricism and rationalism?
2. How is the ideality of space and time compatible with empirical realism, in Kant's view?

TRANSCENDENTAL LOGIC (NKS 92; A50/B74)

The second transcendental element of consciousness is transcendental logic, which as an *a priori* condition of possibility, constitutes the next aspect of our answer to the question of the possibility of synthetic a *priori* knowledge. This distinctive conception of logic is set forth in the Transcendental Analytic, which is the second main division of the First Critique and will be the subject of most of our following exposition, including the sections of the Transcendental Deduction, Transcendental Judgment, the Principles of Pure Reason, and closing with the grand distinction between the Phenomenon and Noumena. And, as suggested above, just as the Transcendental Aesthetic set out an *a priori* doctrine of pure sensibility, the section on transcendental logic sets forth a doctrine of pure understanding. As we will see, it is the synthetic unity of both of these elements of consciousness which will describe the entire field of an active, representational consciousness, or, in shorthand, of the phenomenon.

In order to understand the significance of *transcendental* logic for Kantian philosophy, and in order to comprehend its peculiarity with respect to the conception of logic set forth by rationalists such as Leibniz, it is necessary to distinguish it from formal logic, or, from that which Kant calls *general* logic. The latter can be described as that logic which concerns analytic truth, and can be represented most immediately in the tautology of the first law of logic, that of identity. This type of logic, being analytic, is self-referential and concerns the disclosure of the contents of the subject of the proposition as they are stated in the predicate. In this type of logic, as we have seen above, nothing new is added by the predicate, e.g. 'All bodies are extended'. Transcendental logic on the other hand, as synthetic, does seek to state something *new under the sun*, something which is not included in the subject of the proposition, e.g. 'All bodies are heavy'.

However, as a logic which is not merely meant to rely on the empirical realm for verification, it must say something 'new' that is synthetic and *a priori*. It is upon the basis of this transcendental logic that, for Kant, all theoretical science depends. This is a logic which seeks to make *a priori* statements about the world, one which is neither content to remain inside of its windowless domain in a mere play amongst concepts, nor in a mere re-articulation of the laws of logic or reduction of the world to various expressions of these laws, such as is carried in symbolic logic. This point is important since if we merely followed the former course, logic would remain irrelevant to the world, and if we followed the latter course, logic would be a violent imposition upon the world. As we will see, in the Transcendental Deduction Kant is concerned with the justice of our use of concepts to describe the world, and any logic, if it is to be *de juris*, must demonstrate its *right* and remain, as its own most proper domain, within the conditions of possibility of experience. In this light, that which Kant seeks is a logic which *transcends to the world*, and indeed, which allows the phenomenon to disclose or express itself as the object of our own experience.

In this way, a transcendental logic will disclose itself as that condition of possibility, along with that of sensibility, which is the ground for the orchestration of objects in the manifold of experience. Both of these conditions are after all necessary, for sensibility without the concept would be, for Kant, merely *blind*, and conceptuality with intuition would be *empty*. It is the *unity* of these transcendental conditions which makes experience, and synthetic *a priori* knowledge, possible.

Kant sets forth twelve such concepts of transcendental logic in his famous (and for some, like Heidegger, infamous) Table of Concepts. These twelve concepts, which he considers to have the character of uniqueness, completeness and necessity are further divided into four divisions: Quantity, Quality, Relation and Modality. These divisions all have three concepts under them as set out in the following schema:

Quantity	*Quality*
Unity	Reality
Plurality	Negation
Totality	Limitation

Relation	*Modality*
Inherence and Subsistence	Possibility and Impossibility
Causality and Dependence	Existence and Non-existence
Community	Necessity and Contingency

These concepts are the ontological and phenomenological prerequisites for any being to have existence in the world and each division describes the being of the world from its own necessary perspective. Each of these aspects of being must be able to be distinguished and looked at separately in order to have a complete theoretical exposition of the being of any object. Moreover, each grouping of concepts builds internally upon the preceding in an almost syllogistic fashion.

An example is in order. Let us take the example of acorns setting underneath an oak tree in Aristotle's *Physics*. From the perspective of Quantity, we may state *in abstraction* that there is a single acorn, which exists in its singularity as a Unity. At the same time, we may also state that there are many acorns, which while possessing unity in each of themselves, form a Plurality of the type 'acorns'. Finally, with respect to the category of Quantity, the Unity and the Plurality of acorns constitute the Totality of the type of phenomenon designated by the term 'acorn'.

With respect to Quality, we could state that each acorn has its own kind of being or existence, its Reality. Moreover, we could state, when surveying the plurality of acorns around this particular one (while not considering, however, quantity as quantity), that this one is different from the others, that it is the Negation of the others with respect to its own particular manifestation. Finally, with respect to the category of Quality, we could state that the unity of the Reality and Negation of the acorns sets out the concept of Limitation of each acorn with respect to the rest of the others in terms of its own particular manifestation.

With respect to the concepts of Relation, we could state that each acorn Subsists in itself, as it is, (which is not the same as having a Quality or Quantity distinct from the others), but Inheres in a particular situation. Moreover, if, for instance, during a gust of wind or with the flight of a raven, an acorn falls, hitting another, we could state that the relationship between the being of one acorn and that of another is that of Causality and Dependence. And, if we then synthesise these concepts, there emerges a Community of subsistent beings in their specific interaction.

The fourth division of concepts, of Modality, is slightly different as it concerns the mode of being of the object under consideration, and in this way, most clearly resembles the analysis of the development of the acorn as set out in Aristotle's *Physics*. In this way, we will consider the Possibility, Existence and Necessity of the type of being which is an acorn. This way of looking at the acorn, distinct from that of Quantity, Quality, and Relation, will consider how an acorn *exists*. We will first consider that which is *possible* for the acorn, in this instance, that of growing into an oak tree and not a horse, which is *impossible*. We will next consider the prerequisites or conditions for its Existence, which are necessary for it to be, as opposed to that state in which it would have Non-existence. Finally, we will consider the unity of Possibility and Existence in the resulting Necessity or Contingency of the actualisation of its Existence as emerging from Possibility. In terms of its way of being or of its mode of existence, there is a great gulf between possibility and existence. We know that which it can be, and that which is required for it to be in this way, and it is from this reflection that we begin to comprehend what is necessary and what is contingent.

While there may have been other (and perhaps better) examples for the relevance of the concepts to an object of experience, it is clear that if we look at the world in a transcendental manner, we at once realise the complexity of any seemingly naïve object of experience (as set forth by Hume). Any 'thing' that we may experience can suddenly be illuminated in light of this conceptual schema. A classroom, society, or an artwork, for instance: the quantity of students, citizens or aspects, their qualities, their relations, and the way of being of the group, its state or composition as such. Moreover, we can ascertain the difference between this type of logic and that of formal logic which circles self-referentially around differing expressions of the law of identity. Transcendental logic is different to the extent that it explicitly seeks to *step out into the world* and to set out the conceptual conditions of possibility of experience itself.

For Kant, this categorical table serves, along with that of pure sensibility, as a transcendental ground for experience, a table which abides in our active consciousness and which is projected to constitute the organisational structure of the world, *as we know it.* It will be the question of the Transcendental Deduction if we indeed have this right, or instead if our concepts are merely *usurpations*, or in other words, violent assertions upon, and indeed, against experience. For Kant, it is the unity of sensibility and understanding which constitutes the 'world', the 'phenomenon', and answers the question of the possibility of synthetic *a priori* judgments.

At this point, I would like to summarise my preceding explication of the two transcendental elements of our active, projective consciousness and show how the unification of these constitutes the phenomenon of the 'world' of representation. In order to facilitate a more simple understanding of the complexity of our experience, something that, as we have seen, is not that simple at all, I will lay out the following schema or flow-chart:

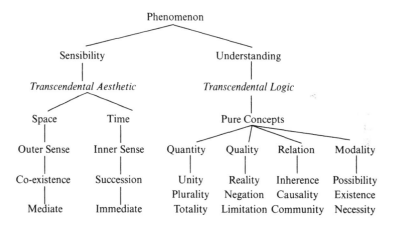

As we can see from this schema, the *phenomenon* is nothing but *complex* (and from now on, when I refer to the 'phenomenon', I will be using the term as shorthand for this complex analysis of 'experience'). It is *not* the simple object of the empiricists. At the same time, Kant is not simply trying to sequester the truths of fact from those of reason as he is laying out the transcendental conditions of possibility of experience in the faculties of sensibility and the understanding. However, as I have suggested, the possibility of unity between sensibility and understanding, and thus of knowledge, lies upon the synthesis of the *pure* imagination. 'Experience' emerges for the first time from an act of imagination. In this light, we will continue our reading of the First *Critique*, in the Transcendental Logic, but with particular notice given to the uncanny guest of imagination (in what was to be a section on logic), which I will disclose, as being the third basic faculty of the soul, and thus as the root of *a priori* synthetic knowledge.

Study questions

1. How does Kant identify the pure concepts of the understanding? To what extent is his approach open to question?
2. What is the difference between formal or general logic and transcendental logic? How is this difference related to the Copernican Revolution?

IMAGINATION, SYNTHESIS AND THE THIRD BASIC FACULTY OF THE SOUL

If there is to be an *a priori* synthetic judgment, sensibility must make a connection with the understanding. Once again, we are not asking if such judgments exist, but, instead, how they are at all possible. We have seen how the ideality of space and time, as pure intuitions, serves as one of the necessary conditions for the possibility for synthetic *a priori* judgments. Moreover, Kant, in the Transcendental Logic, lays out the second necessary condition of possibility in an examination of the faculty of understanding and of its pure concepts (categories). In the case of the concept, it is logic, in contrast to aesthetic, that makes up the canon of rules for thought, for the understanding and for its judgment.

Kant describes two stems of knowledge in the Introduction to the *Critique of Pure Reason*, a distinction of sensibility and understanding which becomes ever more elaborate as we examine the relationship between the two stems. We will find that the explication of this relationship necessitates an examination of the primary role of the imagination in the grounding of synthetic *a priori* judgments. In other words, through a consideration of the relationship between the faculties of sensibility and understanding, and of the transcendental distance which separates them, we will begin to comprehend the necessity of a third primary faculty of knowledge, but one which neither be a root, nor a stem of knowledge.[7]

Sensibility, which deals with intuition, has the character of receptivity, as that which apprehends that which is given, whether as a pure intuition or an empirical intuition. The understanding, on the other hand, which deals with the concept, has the character of spontaneity, of the act of thought. As these two are linked together, as receptive spontaneity, or spontaneous receptivity, there exists the state by which a synthetic *a priori* judgment became possible. It is a union of opposites, each of which is incomplete without the other. Kant writes:

> Intuition and concepts constitute, therefore, the elements of all our knowledge, so that neither concepts without an intuition in some way corresponding to them, nor intuition without concepts, can yield knowledge. (NKS 92; A50, B74)

Kant writes further, regarding the status of the faculties, each to the other:

> To neither of these powers may a preference be given over the other. Without sensibility no object would be given to us, without understanding no object would be thought. Thoughts without content are empty, intuitions without concepts are blind. (NKS 93; A51, B75)

Kant concludes: 'Only through their union can knowledge arise'. (NKS 93; A51, B75) The possibility of such a union depends upon a possible relation between sensibility and concepts, in the sense of a logos of being. But to this extent, Kant must return to logic in order to ascertain the conceptuality which will allow for a unity with sensibility.

For Kant, logic must be divided into two divisions, general and transcendental. It is the latter division which will be of primary concern with regard to the question of the possibility of synthetic *a priori* judgments. But it is the former division, that of general logic, especially in its pure form, which gives us an important clue. Kant writes that in pure general logic,

> we abstract from all empirical conditions under which our understanding is exercised, i.e., from the influence of the senses, the

play of imagination, the laws of memory, the force of habit, inclination, etc., and so from all sources of prejudice, indeed from all causes from which this or that knowledge may arise or seem to arise. (NKS 94; A52–53, B77)

Pure general logic is abstracted from body and from world. And, it is from the imagination, once again, that the purity of knowledge has fled, or, at least has distanced from itself in a radical way. However, if there is to be a union of concept and intuition, and hence, a demonstration of the possibility of synthetic *a priori* judgments, there is required a logic which is capable of thinking an object, but in a manner which retains its *a priori* status. Kant writes:

> In that case we should have a logic in which we do not abstract from the entire content of knowledge. This other logic, which should contain solely the rules of the pure thought of an object, would exclude only those modes of knowledge which have empirical content. (NKS 95; A55, B80)

Transcendental logic concerns *a priori* knowledge about experience, while not being of, or, arising out of, experience. As with the pure intuitions of space and time, the pure concepts of this other logic are characterised as constituents of the mind, in this case, as acts of thought by which a concept applies its rule to the pure manifold of *a priori* intuition. Kant writes, '. . . it concerns itself with the laws of understanding and of reason solely in so far as they relate *a priori* to objects' (NKS 97; A57, B82). But, while it is necessary to open up a division of logic to the mere possibility of contact with objects, *a priori*, Kant insists that there is a definite limit to the necessary inclusion of the content of experience. He admits that as regards content there is no criteria of truth that will stand, least of all, logic, that will provide a guarantee for the exercise of transcendental logic. And while Kant is not concerned with the content *in concreto*, but, as quoted, only with the mere possibility of an object, this does not mean that he can disregard other criteria or domains of truth.

Logic provides, by means of the principle of contradiction, a *via negativa* of ascertaining truth. This would be adequate if we were considering the realm of logic alone, of pure thought. But, since we are seeking to transcend logic towards objects, to think objects as intuitions via concepts, we must allow a 'positive' truth of the object to 'correct' even logic with respect to synthetic *a priori* knowledge. Otherwise, if we merely remain sequestered in the realm of pure concepts, and presume that the understanding has its own content, or that we can dispense with not only the concrete content of sensibility, but also with space and time as pure intuitions, we 'end in nothing', writes Kant, 'but mere talk', (NKS 99; A61, B86) again flying aloft in the illusions of mere concepts. There must be a horizon of possible experience, for even the mere possible relation of thought to some possible object keeps open a relation to truth (NKS 100; A63, B87).

As intimated in the Transcendental Logic, Kant undertakes a transcendental analytic, as a 'dissection of the faculty of understanding itself. . .' (NKS 103; A65, B90). The goal is to elaborate a complete system of the pure concepts of discursive understanding.[8] Even as he seeks a transcendental logic, Kant still remains tied to formal logic, as seen in his derivation of pure concepts from the logical functions of judgment. It must be kept in mind that this 'other' logic remains connected to general logic proper, to the extent that understanding itself is regarded as the 'faculty of judgment' (NKS 106; A69, B94). Kant writes:

Concepts are based on the spontaneity of thought, sensible intuitions on the receptivity of impressions. Now the only use which the understanding can make of these concepts is to judge by means of them. Since no representation, save when it is an intuition, is in immediate relation to an object, no concept is ever related to an object immediately, but to some other representation of it, be that other representation an intuition, or itself, a concept. Judgment is therefore the mediate knowledge of an object, that is, the representation of a representation of it. (NKS 105; A68, B93)

Judgment, says Kant, is a function of unity among representations. But, it does not touch sensibility, it is not 'immediate'. Kant says that it is a 'higher' representation. A problem seems to be looming on the horizon, an echo of our initial paradox. For, if the concept cannot embrace sensibility directly, and if we are seeking to demonstrate the conditions of possibility for synthetic *a priori* judgments, then there must be some other power, which can serve as a link between sensibility and understanding.

The pure concepts have before themselves a manifold of pure intuition. Yet, this manifold of pure intuition has no value for the concept in its 'raw' condition. Kant writes of the synthesis which organises the manifold: 'But, if this manifold is to be known, the spontaneity of our thought requires that it be gone through in a certain way, taken up, and connected' (NKS 111; A77, B102). And, he continues: 'By *synthesis*, in its most general sense, I understand the act of putting different representations together, and of grasping what is manifold in them in one act of knowledge' (NKS 111; A77, B103). Thus, a synthesis of the manifold of space and time engenders the mediate representation which is given to the concept, and thus is 'what first gives rise to our knowledge' (NKS 111; A78, B103). Kant writes:

> This knowledge may, indeed, at first, be crude and confused, and therefore in need of analysis. Still the synthesis is that which gathers the elements for knowledge, and unites them to form a certain content. It is to synthesis, therefore, that we must first direct our attention, if we would determine the first origin of our knowledge. (NKS 111–112; A78, B103)

What we require for an answer to the question of synthetic *a priori* judgments is a synthesis of the manifold which will transfigure the rhapsody of pure intuition into a 'certain content', that 'content' which must be somehow available to the understanding. By means of such a synthesis, the possibility of synthetic knowledge is linked to the necessity of an autonomous (pure) discursive understanding which must remain detached from the temporal priority of pure intuition. Kant announces the answer we seek:

> Synthesis in general, as we shall hereafter see, is the mere result of the power of imagination, a blind but indispensable function of the soul, without which we should have no knowledge whatsoever, but of which we are scarcely ever conscious. To bring this synthesis **to concepts** is a function which belongs to the understanding, and it is through this function of the understanding that we first obtain knowledge properly so called. (NKS 112; A78, B103)

It is thus the imagination which brings a 'certain content' to the otherwise empty concept. This admission is somewhat ironic considering the lengths Kant has so far gone, and would eventually go, to isolate the imagination from the kingdom of pure, *a priori* knowledge. We can even hear in this immediate act of imagination echoes of his polemic against Leibniz and Wolff. For, we will recall, Kant describes the synthetic imagination in relation to Leibniz in the early pages of the First *Critique*:

> framing out of the relations abstracted from experience something that does indeed contain what is general in these relations, but which cannot exist without the restrictions which nature has attached to them. (NKS 81; A40, B57)

What is missing, however, from this contingent knowledge, of this 'certain content', is apodeictic certainty, that *logical criteria of truth* that allows a knowledge to be considered strict, necessary and universal.[9] Thus, this operation of synthetic framing is admitted in so far as it organises a manifold as a pure synthesis of representations '. . . executed according to a common ground of unity' (NKS 112; A78, B104). The *empirical,* reproductive, imagination stands in between sensibility and understanding as an operation of knowledge, a function of the soul, but is itself insufficient for the creation of proper knowledge. Kant writes:

> What must first be given – with a view to the *a priori* knowledge of all objects – is the *manifold* of pure intuition; the second factor involved is the *synthesis* of this manifold by means of the imagination. But even this does not yield knowledge. The concepts which give *unity* to this pure synthesis, and which consist solely in the representation of this necessary synthetic unity, furnish the third requisite for the knowledge of an object; and they rest on the understanding. (NKS 112; A78–79, B104)

This gives us a preliminary answer to our question: there are two stems, or sources of our knowledge; and the stems, or sources, are brought together by the synthetic actions of the imagination. But, can we not detect a great difficulty here?

If the imagination is only a creature of sensibility, and hence of the *a posteriori,* how can it play the mediating role that it does with respect to the faculties? Must it not be a sort of hybrid of the sensible and the intellectual, if it is to be a condition of mediation betwixt them? And, if the imagination is capable of transcendental, and hence, *a priori* employment, would that not force us to revise Kant's initial characterisation of the imagination as an creature of experience, of the *a posteriori*? For if not, then what will then serve to explain the central mediating role of the imaginative synthesis? We will begin to consider these and other questions in an exposition of Transcendental Deduction, A and B. For, it is precisely in the question of the right of pure concepts to be applied themselves to the manifold of experience that the manner in which this application is carried out will come under much scrutiny. It is in this context, that the question of imagination, and its possible *a priori* employment, will assume centre stage.

Study questions

1. To what extent is the imagination the answer to the question: 'How are synthetic *a priori* judgments possible?'?
2. What difficulties arise for the Kantian project with the designation of imagination as a third basic faculty? Is there a solution to the question of imagination in the context of the Kantian project?

TRANSCENDENTAL DEDUCTION: A AND B EDITIONS
(NKS 120; A84/B116)

Introduction: The Meaning of the Transcendental Deduction
Echoing his earlier exclusion of empirical representation from the domain of the *a priori*, Kant states there must be a *transcendental deduction* of the pure concepts of understanding, with respect to the question of the legitimacy of the application of pure concepts in an *a priori* manner, to empirical objects. He writes: 'This demand for a deduction involves us in considerable perplexity, no clear legal title, sufficient to justify their employment, being obtainable either from experience or from reason' (NKS 120;A84–85, B117). Kant repeatedly emphasises the distinction between his proof of legitimacy and inquiries which seek, as with Locke, a 'de facto mode of origination' (NKS 121;A85, B117). Conspicuously, Kant distances himself from the inquiry he calls a 'physiological derivation', which derives the concept from experience. For Kant, however, the deduction of the concepts is not concerned with 'occasioning causes of their production' (NKS 121;A85, B118). That does not mean that Kant is

unaware of these 'causes'. However, he insists that the task of the *Critique* differs from a genealogy in that the former is concerned with right and not with fact, for the latter is excluded by the criteria of necessity and universality. A genealogy is a contingent knowledge, and as with the empirical imagination, inductively frames general relations of experience. Kant does not dismiss this knowledge as such. Indeed, he briefly engages in a 'physiological derivation' of his own with respect to those 'first strivings of human knowledge': 'The impressions of the senses supplying the first stimulus, the whole faculty of knowledge opens out to them, and experience is brought into existence' (NKS 121; A86, B118). Kant is not troubled by this knowledge, as we also remember from his attitude to the inductive, collocative imagination, which had an immediate access to objects, already there amidst objects. The issue remains, nevertheless, as necessary within the critical endeavour, one of legitimacy, to establish the 'legal right' of a web of concepts which already dominate, but may have attained their supremacy through usurpation. Kant, as we have seen, accepts this usurpation and the *de facto* existence of the sciences; he accepts the crime of Prometheus. Yet, it is his task to reflect upon this knowledge in order to establish a grounding via a deduction which *must establish* both the purity of the concept, and its relation to the object of experience in an *a priori* manner.

Kant admits that this *apology* for the pure concepts will be difficult to construct since the ambiguity of the concept has aroused suspicion as to its 'objective validity and the limits of its employment' (NKS 123; A88, B120). In other words, since the concept cannot, out of itself, engender an object upon which it would ground its synthesis, it must enter into relation with possible experience, as that is its horizon of affectivity. Yet, even as these concepts are reaching out to experience, they must display an origin all of their own, 'to show a certificate of birth quite other than that of descent from experience' (NKS 122; A86–87, B119).[10] Pure intuitions, which 'contain *a priori* the condition of the possibility of objects as appearances' and through a synthesis of the imagination, engender the manifold. In this, pure intuition retains an intimacy with experience. However, pure concepts must remain at a distance from experience, must not be the condition for the *emergence* of objects of experience. Nor, on the other hand, do objects need to conform to the understanding, unless of course, we are seeking *a priori* knowledge (NKS 123; A89, B121).

The initial question, 'How are synthetic *a priori* judgments possible?' therefore becomes, 'How are subjective conditions of thought to have objective validity?' In a tone of ironic alarm, Kant suggests that it is 'not at all obvious' that we must affirm the legitimacy of the pure concepts. He even engages in a quasi-Cartesian thought experiment, describing a 'possible' a-conceptual world:

> Appearances might very well be so constituted that the understanding should not find them to be in accordance with the conditions of its unity. Everything might be in such a confusion that, for instance, in the series of appearances nothing presented itself which might yield a rule of synthesis and so answer to the concept of cause and effect. This concept would then be altogether empty, null, and meaningless. But since intuition stands in no need whatsoever of the functions of thought, appearances would none the less present objects to our intuition. (NKS 124; A90–91, B123)

This possibility of 'non-intelligibility' (and indeed of nihilism) is that which stimulates Kant to undertake the transcendental investigation. Kant describes the fate of the confused inquirer who avoids this Deduction: 'Otherwise he proceeds blindly, and after manifold wanderings must come back to the same ignorance from which he started' (NKS 123; A88, B121). Kant suggests further that if this deduction is not possible, then concepts must be '. . . given up as a mere phantom of the brain' (NKS 125; A91, B123). What we can gather from this thought experiment is his admission that there is a modality of empirical knowledge which proceeds by virtue of the 'blind, but indispensable' power of imagination, and not (yet) by means of the concept. However, pure knowledge must remain ultimately the 'proper' condition for the possibility of empirical knowledge. And Kant suggests that the criteria for this proper knowledge is, once again, the 'strict universality of the rule' (NKS 125; A91, B124). This strictness of the rule implies a plane of concepts at a distance from experience, and it is to this distance which Kant ascribes 'dignity' (NKS 125; A91, B124).

Towards a resolution of the paradox, and thus to obtain an answer to his question, Kant sets up a decision: 'Either the object alone must make the representation possible or the representation alone must make the object possible' (NKS 125; A92, B124–5). Once again, in a re-statement of the Copernican Revolution, Kant sets up a contrast between concept and intuition, the two stems or sources of knowledge, and of the relations between these stems. In that his central focus remains the question of the validity of the concept, and of its apodeictic certainty, he remarks that only the latter option will yield *a priori* knowledge, that the concept, as a pure representation, must make the object possible. Moreover, the seeming clarity of the decision to be made allows him to translate the question as follows: 'The question now arises whether *a priori* concepts do not also serve as antecedent conditions under which alone anything can be, if not intuited, yet thought as object in general' (NKS 126; A93, B125). If Kant can establish that these concepts are indeed the conditions under which empirical objects are possible, then it will be shown that, even if objects may appear without apparent relationship to the functions of the understanding, all empirical knowledge would be dependent upon the web of *a priori* concepts. And, since there is no genuine alarm about this *a priori* determination of concepts, he simply asserts that empirical knowledge must be grounded upon pure concepts of understanding. Kant reiterates his distinction between a physiological induction and a transcendental deduction:

> Concepts which yield the objective ground of the possibility of experience are for this very reason necessary. But the unfolding of the experience wherein they are encountered is not their deduction; it is only their illustration. For on any such exposition they would be merely accidental. Save through their original relation to possible experience, in which all objects of knowledge are found, their relation to any one object would be quite incomprehensible. (NKS 126–127; A94, B126–127)

This distinction between a *deduction* and an *illustration* plays itself out in a controversial revision made by Kant between the First (1781) and Second Edition (1787) of the *Critique of Pure Reason*, specifically that of the excised A94–95, which is displaced by B127–129, a text which further pursues the above distinction. This revision plays a significant role not only in the work of the German Idealists but also in Heidegger's destructive interpretation of the Kantian revisions – and hence, of the meaning of the *Critique* itself. For now we will briefly consider the excision of A94 as a prelude to a consideration of the status and role of the imagination in each of the two Deductions. The excised passage (NKS 127; A94–95) is as follows:

> There are three original sources (capacities or faculties of the soul) which contain the conditions of the possibility of all experience, and cannot themselves be derived from any other faculty of the mind, namely *sense, imagination,* and *apperception.* Upon them are grounded (1) the *synopsis* of the manifold *a priori* through sense; (2) the *synthesis* of this manifold through imagination; finally (3) the *unity* of this synthesis through original apperception. All these *faculties* have a transcendental (as well as empirical) employment which concerns the form alone, and is possible *a priori.* As regards sense, we have treated of this above in the first part; we shall now endeavour to comprehend the nature of the other two.

This passage accords with A78–9, B104, considered above with respect·to *three* necessary constituents of *a priori* knowledge. However, as suggested, it merely echoes the questions of the relation of the imagination to the other two sources or stems of knowledge. This would also, in this context, be a question of the status and character of the faculty of imagination amidst a strict distinction between the sensible and the intelligible, one made more severe in the B Edition. Moreover, the possibility, laid out in the A Deduction, of a transcendental and *a priori* power of the imagination raises problems with respect to the characterisation of the imagination as merely a creature of sensibility.

The revised passages, the addition of B127–29, reiterate the distinction between a deduction and a physiological derivation, or illustration. Kant fashions (through his translator) a pun upon 'illustration', introducing Locke and Hume as illustrious men. They both derive concepts from experience, and each therefore forsakes strict universality and necessity with respect to knowledge as such. Once again, Kant is not denying that they have *a* knowledge. However, he is emphatic in his assertion that their knowledge will remain only contingent. Yet, Kant himself may not be worthy of such confidence in that he has been visited by the uncanny guest of the imagination as the third, as the in between, a power which by being neither one stem of knowledge nor the other, neither intuition nor concept, injects ambiguity into what was at first sight a very simple and clear cut decision between the concept and experience. Such ambiguity, cast into relief by the metaphor of an unknown root à la Hamann and Heidegger, not only threatens the project of grounding the legitimacy of the pure concepts in their application to experience, but also that of an extension of knowledge beyond experience, one which requires the utmost care in the original explication of first principles. We will now turn to the A Deduction to consider its treatment of the imagination.

Imagination in the A Deduction (NKS 129; A95)

In the A Deduction, Kant seeks to answer his earlier question of the relation between the two stems of pure, *a priori* knowledge, sensibility and understanding. He seeks to 'render comprehensible this relation of understanding to sensibility, and by means of sensibility, to all objects of experience' (NKS 149; A128). That is, he seeks to establish that there is such a relation which would allow for an *a priori* determination of sensibility via pure concepts of understanding, in other words, that only through a concept 'can an object be thought' (NKS 130; A96–97). This possibility is made comprehensible through a further consideration of the three subjective sources of *a priori* knowledge, which were considered above with respect to A79, B103, and A94–95.

Kant, in section three of the Deduction, informs his reader that the 'two extremes' sensibility and understanding are brought into relation by 'the mediation of this transcendental function of imagination. . .' (NKS 146; A124). Yet, this innocuous word 'mediation' does not begin to allow us to grasp the necessary role that imagination plays in the grounding of *a priori* knowledge. However, the term 'mediation' remains significant in another way in that it implies that imagination possesses, as an *a priori* principle, facultative independence.[11] If this were not the case, the word 'mediation' would indeed have no meaning. Could principles mediate through a conduit which was not *pure*?

In the Preliminary Remark (NKS 131–137; A98–110), Kant begins to exhibit the complexities of this 'mediation' produced by the imagination. He echoes his earlier discussion of transcendental logic when he invokes a spontaneity upon which sets a 'threefold synthesis', of apprehension, of reproduction, and of recognition. It might seem that the imagination, with its ambiguous status, has been placed safely in the middle, as with Aristotle, in his *De Anima*, concerned with 'merely' reproducing the unity of the manifold of appearance at the behest of the concept and sensation. Yet, this would be to overlook the originative enactment of *pure* imagination. This implies of course an *a priori*, transcendental status, that has been admitted already by Kant.

In other words, the emphasis only upon an empirical, reproductive operation of imagination, prohibits a clear consideration of the entire activity of the 'transcendental faculty of imagination' (NKS 133; A102). A single example will show us that we must exercise care in our interpretation. Kant writes with regard to the first source of knowledge: 'But to such a synopsis a synthesis must always correspond; receptivity can make knowledge possible only when combined with spontaneity' (NKS 130; A97). One might, if the imagination was to be considered only from an empirical, reproductive standpoint, designate this spontaneity in this case as apperception. Yet, it is the blind imagination which engenders synthetic connection, and this synthesis *is* spontaneity with respect to the receptivity of the synopsis. It may be therefore the spontaneity of the productive imagination which is meant in this case. Or is apperception that to which Kant alludes? For Kant next relates that this spontaneity is the ground of a threefold synthesis: apprehension, reproduction and recognition, each of which corresponds to the 'three subjective sources of knowledge, which make possible the understanding itself. . .' (NKS 131; A97). We will defer a clarification of this question until later.

As Kant has related, each of the sources of knowledge has an empirical and a transcendental capacity. It is the latter grounding character which serves as an *a priori* condition of knowledge. But, to each of these sources must correspond a synthesis. And since the power of synthesis belongs to the 'blind' imagination, this latter source has a unique relationship to apprehension, reproduction and also recognition.

In the synthesis of apprehension, it is time which is the receptacle of all representations, via which they are 'ordered, connected, and brought together' (NKS 131; A98). We suspect that a singular representation, as it occurs in a single moment (*Augenblick*), holds within itself absolute unity. Yet, our intuition already contains a manifold due to the proliferation of temporal moments, and thus, there is absolute multiplicity. To fathom the unity we suspect, the manifold must be 'run through, and held together. . .' by means of a synthesis that is 'directed immediately upon intuition. . .' (NKS 131; A99).

We soon grasp that this synthesis of apprehension is the work of the transcendental imagination[12] (Heidegger describes a *syndosis* of the imagination in his 1927 lecture course, *Phenomenological Interpretation of Kant's Critique of Pure Reason*) when in a rather enigmatic statement Kant says that this intuition 'does indeed offer a manifold, but a manifold which can never be represented as a manifold, and as contained *in a single representation*, save in virtue of this synthesis' (NKS 131–132; A99).

The imagination thus has an immediate relation to intuition via its involvement in apprehension and its synthesis, but a relation which compels it to 'conceal' what it has apprehended. Indeed, the single moment of intuition cannot be represented since the imagination, in its *reproductive synthesis*, represents and reproduces the play of difference which is inherent in the temporal association of ordered multiplicity. That which is original in the singular moment of vision, in apprehension, is thus akin to a myth, *poiesis*, always displaced by the production and reproduction of the synthetic manifold (NKS 133; A102). Yet, *poiesis* as the synthesis of reproduction is in turn grounded upon the transcendental synthesis of imagination, 'as conditioning the very possibility of all experience' (NKS 133; A101).

In his consideration of the *synthesis of recognition* in the concept, Kant reminds us that his main concern lies in logical truth and apodeictic certainty. In this context, this concern has transfigured into that of logical identity and the necessity of a unified consciousness, or a formal unity of consciousness, of the numerical identity of the 'I'. The organised series of connected representations may well be generated by the synthetic activity of the imagination, but without a consciousness of the series, it would not 'form a whole', for unity, in the sense of totality, is imparted by consciousness. Yet, could it not be (and does not Kant admit) that it is the transcendental imagination which creates this 'whole', if only in response to the demands of reason for totality.

What the concept contributes to knowledge is to be explained through the distinction between generation and outcome. Kant suggests that the concept need not be involved in the actual generation of representations, but is concerned with the outcome, as it is conscious of the unity of the outcome. It does not itself need to do anything, as it is the visual counterpart to an imagination which exudes a 'blind play of representations, less even than a dream' (NKS 139; A112).[13] He contends that the synthesis of empirical imagination must be grounded upon the transcendental power of imagination, thus providing a rule for the simple coherence of representations. Moreover, he infers that there must be a transcendental ground for the *unity* of this act of the synthesis of representations, and hence, for the transcendental imagination itself. Kant writes:

All necessity, without exception, is grounded in a transcendental condition. There must, therefore, be a transcendental ground of the unity of consciousness in the synthesis of the manifold of all our intuitions, and consequently also of the concepts of objects in general, and so of all objects of experience, a ground without which it would be impossible to think any object for our intuitions; for this object is no more than that something, the concept of which expresses such a necessity of synthesis. (NKS 135–136; A106)

Kant designates this ground as transcendental apperception, which is a 'pure original unchangeable consciousness' (NKS 136; A107). He further writes: 'To render such a transcendental presupposition valid, there must be a condition which precedes all experience, and which makes experience itself possible' (NKS 136; A107). He declares that the [numerical] unity of apperception is the *a priori* ground of all concepts, just as pure intuition is the *a priori* ground of sensibility. Transcendental apperception is thus not merely an inspector of the work of the imagination, but is its original instigator and commander. Kant alleges that consciousness may 'often be only faint, so that we do not connect it with the act itself. . .' (NKS 134; A103). But, the unity of apperception is always there as the consciousness which initially envisages a synthetic manifold and allows it into our knowledge. This manifold, synthesised and represented for consciousness by imagination is the outcome that allows the self an intimation of its hidden truth. He writes:

For the mind could never think its identity in the manifoldness of its representations, and indeed think this identity *a priori*, if it did not have before its eyes the identity of its act, whereby it subordinates all synthesis of apprehension (which is empirical) to a transcendental unity, thereby rendering possible their interconnection according to *a priori* rules. (NKS 137; A108)

To this apperception corresponds the transcendental object to which a manifold of synthetic experience must be ultimately related with respect to the necessity of a relation of knowledge to a referent. We are not to know this object, for only appearances are immediate, but must however assume the necessity of its existence, and think beyond the web of representations. Kant writes:

> This relation is nothing but the necessary unity of consciousness, and therefore also of the synthesis of the manifold, through a common function of the mind, which combines it in one representation. (NKS 137; A109)

Yet, once again we must be careful in our interpretation of this claim that we know nothing about this transcendental object, or of that which transcends the labyrinth of conscious representations. According to the theoretical criteria for proper knowledge, as that which exhibits universality and necessity, we do not know things, and must forsake such a knowledge, for knowledge must be *a priori*, and hence, is possible only if we consider appearances to be merely the web of our own representations. Yet, we have already seen that the imagination acts inductively and synthetically amidst objects (and represents to us that which is not *present*), but, as we are within the strictures of the Kantian *a priori*, and inside his representational theory of consciousness, we are thereby forbidden to consider, with Husserl and Heidegger, the 'things themselves'.

In this phenomenological sense, the imagination would not be simply a 'mediator' between sense and understanding, but would open up an intentional space, where there would be a mode of transcendence of consciousness amidst phenomena, as the 'things themselves', and not, according to the Kantian framework, as mere appearances. For Kant, we do not 'know' that which is not given to the concept, but we can and may think of these things in the sense of the 'first strivings' of any knowing, or, as the 'coherent content' of the synthesis of representations, which is given to the concept. But, this is not knowledge in the strictest sense, for all knowledge, as Kant writes, 'demands a concept' (NKS 135; A106). Thus, imagination, as it is harnessed to perform work on behalf of the concept, has the status of a 'common function of the mind', as a standing reserve of ubiquitous, but blind activity.

The primacy, for Kant, of the concept and of consciousness is underlined in his assertion that there is one single experience in which all perceptions are represented as in 'thoroughgoing and orderly connection, just as there is only one space and one time in which all modes of appearance and all relation of being and not being occur' (NKS 138; A110). In this passage there is a rejection of the Leibnizian severance of contingency and necessity in the notion of infinite possible worlds. Against Leibniz, Kant asserts that the world which we experience is the only possible world, irrespective of whether or not it is the best.

The proscription of imagination, the fount of possible worlds, as with the exclusion of inductive procedures from the domain of *a priori* knowledge, exposes the discipline which orchestrates the activity of the imagination through the directives of the concept. As Kant explains later in the First *Critique* in 'The Discipline of Pure Reason':

> If the imagination is not simply to be visionary, but is to be inventive under the strict surveillance of reason, there must always previously be something that is completely certain, and not invented or merely a matter of opinion, namely, the possibility of the object itself. (NKS 613; A770, B798)

This requirement of the possibility of the object adheres to the logical criteria of apodeictic certainty, with its equation of the conditions of possibility of experience *as such* with the conditions of possibility for the objects of experience. Or, there can be no escape from the surveillance of reason, for even in the situation of an intuition which severed its ties with experience and consciousness, and thus persisted without necessity and strict universality, 'all relation of knowledge to objects would fall away' (NKS 138; A111). This is not merely a refusal to admit the possibility of an 'intuition without thought', but is an exclusion of such intuition from knowledge (in the strict sense) on principle. For Kant, an intuition without concept would be without an object, and thus would be 'merely a blind play of representations, less even than a dream' (NKS 139; A112).

In *section three* of the Deduction, in which Kant performs the deduction proper, he again suggests that the manner of presentation in the previous Remark was not to be confused with a physiological derivation of the concepts from experience. On the contrary, he writes that a systematic presentation of the deduction must begin and end with the ultimacy of transcendental apperception, self-consciousness; with the notions of unity and numerical identity, which constitute the affinity of the manifold of experience, and are thus the grounds of the possibility not only of knowledge as such, but also of 'nature' itself. Kant writes:

> We are conscious *a priori* of the complete identity of the self in respect of all representations which can ever belong to our knowledge, as being a necessary condition of the possibility of all representations. (NKS 141–142; A116)

Knowledge, then, is a vast connection of representations into one consciousness, and its necessary identity is a condition of its existence. Kant also acknowledges the imagination since it remains the work of this latter power to synthetically originate and reproduce the manifold of intuition. He writes:

> This synthetic unity presupposes *or* [my emphasis] includes a synthesis, and if the former is to be *a priori* necessary, the synthesis must also be *a priori*. The transcendental unity of apperception thus relates to the pure synthesis of imagination, as an *a priori* condition of the possibility of all combination of the manifold in one knowledge. But only the *productive* synthesis of the imagination can take place *a priori*; the reproductive rests upon empirical conditions. (NKS 142–143; A118)

The disjunction expressed in the phrase 'presupposes or includes a synthesis' can be fathomed to exhibit the difference between the A and B Deductions. To foreshadow, in the B Deduction, the inclusion of a synthesis within apperception itself is suggested, as any hint of a region of activity outside the strictures of the concept fades along with any authentic independence of productive imagination. In the new formulation, the power of combination becomes that of the understanding. In the A edition, on the contrary, it is suggested that *apperception itself must depend upon a presupposition of the imaginative synthesis.* As Kant writes, in a sentence with controversial implications (NKS 143; A118):

Thus the principle of the necessary unity of pure (productive) synthesis of imagination, prior to apperception, is the ground of the possibility of all knowledge, especially of experience.

This proposition seems to harbour the implication that apperception, the seat of unity, could necessarily presuppose imagination for its own act of spontaneity, that there is no apperception without synthetic fabrication via imagination. But, this is not to suggest that the imagination could be a candidate for the origin of the concepts or of consciousness itself, as Heidegger would. For, within the parameters of the Kantian *a priori*, even if all the work is done by the power of imagination, the alpha and omega of knowledge, in the strict sense, must be the *unity* of apperception, a self-consciousness that is conceived as having its origin in 'something different' from experience.

Thus, the imagination, from this *logical standpoint* deals only with that which is, in the strict sense, nothing. Moreover, for Kant in the B Deduction, there is not a transcendental imagination which has an integrity independent of the concept, as imagination acquires its transcendental status only in its relation to apperception. Kant moves to remove any trace of the power of imagination as independent in any meaningful way. However, even if the revised B Deduction has presented the Deduction in a systematic way (thus removing the random groping, which he likens to the Egyptians), the discrepancy remains as to the status of imagination vis-à-vis the understanding, not to mention the question of the primacy of imagination as such.[14]

Returning to the A Deduction, but keeping this latter in view, the transcendental imagination may be subordinated to *unity* as the command and incitement of apperception, yet it seems to have a more original relation with apperception than does understanding, a mere faculty of rules and 'birth place' of concepts. Kant throws us into confusion (if we remain merely in the B Deduction):

> *The unity of apperception in relation to the synthesis of imagination* is the *understanding*; and this same unity, with reference to the *transcendental synthesis* of the imagination, the *pure understanding*. (NKS 143; A119)

In many respects, this is an astounding claim by Kant. This would seem to suggest that the imagination, in both of its employments, is an original presupposition for the faculty of concepts. Kant has already suggested this earlier in the disjunctive phrase. In this way, Kant seeks to demonstrate, in *this* Deduction, a relation of concepts and the synthesis of representations, a deduction that seems to rely upon the originary power of imagination. Kant shows us the means by which he has achieved his solution:

> In the understanding there are then pure *a priori* modes of knowledge which contain the necessary unity of the pure synthesis of imagination in respect of all possible appearances. These are the *categories*, that is, the pure concepts of understanding. (NKS 143; A119)

Once again, Kant saves the purity of the concepts from any question of physiological origination. Apperception, the understanding, the affectivity of the concepts, may presuppose or contain the synthetic activity of imagination, but this again is mock heroics, as it is the former which 'must be added to pure imagination, in order to render its function intellectual' (NKS 146; A124). Imagination is necessary, but, for Kant, despite the possibility of a pure imagination which was not blind, he regards it as essentially fragmentary, concerned with nothing, without the unifying direction of apperception.

The integrity of the pure concepts, grounded in apperception, was never a serious problem. The imagination is activity, for Kant, but an action that is blind, merely generating 'accidental collocations' (NKS 144; A121), even an *affinity* of appearances, but never a knowledge that is proper with the characteristics of absolute necessity and strict universality.[15] Indeed, Kant suggests that we may not even be conscious of these chance dependent collocations, writing, 'For it is only because I ascribe all perceptions to one consciousness (original apperception) that I can say of all perceptions that I am conscious of them' (NKS 145; A122). This echoes the claim made earlier that we are 'scarcely ever conscious' of the synthesis of imagination (NKS 111; A78, B103). Kant is restating that this blind imagination, although it is already deployed at the behest of conscious directives, can be brought to light, to knowledge, via the concept, containing as it does the unity of logical design which must elude this intuitive power. It is in the transcendental character of the pure concept that the possibility of knowledge arises. Yet, is apperception not eroding its own purity through interactions with sense, and the imagination, even if put into transcendental attire? Yet, if it does not prove its relation to an appearance (itself the product of the deployment of synthesis according to the strictures of unity), we could simply charge Kant with the construction of a mere tautology, however elaborate the disguise. Moreover, even if we accept the *quid juris*, what of the *quid facti*, which cannot, if the transcendental distinction of sensibility and intelligibility is to be maintained, be answered?

Imagination in the B Deduction (NKS 151; B130)

Kant prefigures to a great extent the form of the B Edition Deduction in Section 3 of the A Deduction, where he writes that a 'systematic' deduction of the pure concepts of understanding would begin and end with transcendental apperception. Yet, this concern for formal presentation must not distract us from what is certainly different about the B Deduction. Firstly, the B Deduction directs its attention almost exclusively upon the unity of transcendental apperception. No longer are there the myriad traces of the play of imagination which characterise the A Deduction. Indeed, it is not even mentioned until Section 24. Secondly, and with astonishment upon the face of the reader, Kant seems to transfer the power of synthesis to the understanding.[16] He writes with regard to this combination (*conjunctio*) that it is:

> an act of spontaneity of the faculty of representation; and since this faculty, to distinguish it from sensibility, must be entitled understanding, all combination – *be we conscious of it or not*, [my emphasis] be it a combination of the manifold of intuition, empirical or non-empirical, or of various concepts – is an act of the understanding. To this act the general title 'synthesis' may be assigned, as indicating that we cannot represent to ourselves anything as combined and that of all representations *combination* is the only one which cannot be given through objects. Being an act of the self-activity of the subject, it cannot be executed save by the subject itself. (NKS 151–152; B130)

In the A Deduction, we saw that Kant frequently had the habit of attributing to the understanding or to apperception an act which was indeed that of the imagination. But in the B Deduction, there is a procedure of equivocation of imagination and understanding, for example, in the manner of attributing the synthetic act to a vague 'self-activity of the subject'. This notion of the subject in its self-activity, in this case, *stands in the way* of a closer look at the relationship between the principles of imagination and of understanding. We are always already standing in the way of ourselves.

In the A Deduction, as we have seen, Kant makes the distinction between generation and outcome, asserting that his conception of *a priori* knowledge is concerned only with the latter. Thus, in what surely amounts to abbreviation, he calls this synthesis an act of the understanding, for the latter in the end is the ground and command of the outcome. But we 'know' that this is only true with respect to the outcome, and not to which faculty performed the work. Yet, we cannot and must not simply assume that this heuristic strategy of abbreviation is also at work in the B Deduction. For, as we have alluded to before, the B Deduction had decided in favour of containment with respect to synthesis. Kant submerges, or disperses, the synthetic power into his concept of combination: 'But the concept of combination includes, besides the concept of the manifold and of its synthesis, also the concept of the unity of the manifold' (NKS 152; B130–131).

This notion of 'combination' gathers into one operational frame what, in the A Deduction, seemed to be discrete activities that were performed via an independent facultative principle. In the B Deduction, even the hint of any possible disunity or of relations amongst the faculties is displaced by an exposition of a ubiquitous transcendental apperception. Kant writes that this apperception 'contains a synthesis of representations, and is possible only through the consciousness of this synthesis' (NKS 153; B133). Whereas a similar passage in the A Deduction allowed for ambiguity to arise with respect to the status of the respective powers of pure *a priori* knowledge, i.e., imagination and apperception, in this instance, this passage, while it may provoke other questions, does not contain the former ambiguity since the synthesis has lost its status as a presupposition.[17]

What is striking in all of this is the sharp contrast in the respective treatments of the imagination. The usurpation of the imagination and its synthesis is barely concealed in the Leibnizian notion of 'concept containment'. In this context, we will invoke Kant's own earlier question of right (*quid juris*), and inquire whether or not this containment can be shown to be legitimate with respect to the *a priori* imagination.

What is different in the B Deduction is not simply its paucity of mention, but what is said of the imagination when it finally does come to light. A consideration of the treatment of imagination in Section 24 is thus necessary if we are comprehend the meaning of the revisions with respect to the significance of the imagination in its broader references. For instance, the *Critique of Practical Reason* was published in close proximity to the Second Edition of the First *Critique* (1787). In this context, we may be led to assume or suppose that the Second *Critique* would be likely to accord with the presentation of the imagination in the B Deduction. We have already seen that this was the case in our outline above of the *Critique of Practical Reason*.

In Section 24 of the B Deduction, Kant describes the synthetic activity of pure concepts, 'forms of thought' which also contain a synthesis. The synthesis, as with the A Deduction, relates to the unity of apperception, but in B, it is not imagination relating to apperception, but understanding to the latter. Yet, we will recall that, in the A edition, '*The unity of apperception in relation to the synthesis of imagination* is the *understanding*. . .' (NKS 143; A119). In the B edition, however, it is the understanding and its concepts which contain within themselves the power of synthesis (however problematic that may be), as the synthesis of the understanding, which Kant describes as follows:

This synthesis, therefore, is at once transcendental and also purely intellectual. But since there lies in us a certain form of *a priori* sensible intuition, which depends on the receptivity of the faculty of representation (sensibility), the understanding, as spontaneity, is able to determine inner sense through the manifold of given representations, in accordance with the synthetic unity of apperception, and so to think synthetic unity of the apperception of the manifold of *a priori sensible intuition* – that being the condition under which all objects of our human intuition must necessarily stand. (NKS 164; B150)

Kant declares that this spontaneity of understanding alone gives it access to the object of experience in the sense of mere appearance. This gives a different slant on the task 'to render comprehensible this relation of understanding to sensibility, and, by means of sensibility, to all objects of experience', (NKS 149; A128) expressed in the

A Deduction. In the latter, there were mock heroics, which, even if insincere, do exhibit traces of a humility that is implied in the context of a 'tribunal of reason'. In other words, there remains the critical sense that there is a problem to be solved by the Deduction, working with which, Kant testifies in the A Preface, 'cost me the greatest labour – labour, as I hope, not unrewarded' (NKS 12; Axvi). Indeed, the 'mock heroics' was a strategy to excite our interest, but it was also a symptom that there are difficulties involved in the relation of understanding and sensibility. This, of course, alludes to the status of the power of imagination, that which was the bridge which brought the stems together.

The question arises immediately: how did Kant get rid of the problem? Where is the paradox, the perplexity and the question, to which a deduction of the pure concepts was an answer? Or, in other words, how is it that the concept comes to contain the power of synthesis? Has Kant built up an ideal matrix, a regime of 'combination', in which each of the sources that are to be brought together somehow dwell together in some 'pre-established harmony', in which all suspicion of the murky origins of concepts has been silenced? Kant provides plenty of testimony for us to answer these and other questions, in the form of a distinction, mentioned only in the B edition, between 'figurative' and 'intellectual' syntheses. This distinction casts into relief a reigning-in and a diminution of the imagination.

The figurative synthesis (*synthesis speciosa*) is that of the manifold of sensible intuition, analogous to the syntheses of the productive and reproductive imaginations in the A Deduction. The intellectual synthesis (*synthesis intellectualis*), on the other hand, which is the source of the 'combination' at issue, is that 'which is thought in the mere category in respect of the manifold of an intuition in general' (NKS 164; B151). Both of these syntheses have an *a priori* capacity; yet, the figurative synthesis, in its *a priori* capacity, is entitled, Kant writes, the 'transcendental synthesis of the imagination' (NKS 165; B151). He explains this title by means of an unexpected exposition of imagination. He begins: '*Imagination is the faculty of representing in intuition an object that is not itself present*' (NKS 165; B151).

This interpretation harkens back to the synthesis of apprehension, described in the A Deduction. In the latter, we will recall, the imagination, acting immediately upon intuition, offers a 'manifold which can never be represented as a manifold, and as contained *in a single representation*. . .' (NKS 131–132; A99) This synthesis ('save in virtue of such a synthesis') runs through and holds together the manifold in the moment of vision, and it reproduces this unified experience in relation to temporality. Of course, apperception, for Kant, is always in the background in order to fulfil the unity of pure knowledge. But, in the A Deduction, apprehension, an act of imagination, is the 'transcendental ground of knowledge', and thus, is a necessary, *a priori*, function of the soul.

However, Kant changes his tone in the B Deduction. He limits the imagination within subjective parameters, and since it has been defined as an intuitive faculty, relegates it to merely the domain of sensibility. In this way, he recasts the imagination in such a way that it is removed to a distance from the exclusive domain of pure knowledge. However, he must still admit that 'imagination', at least as a 'formal indicator' of a necessary cognitive function, has a transcendental, *a priori* dimension. Yet, his admission only exacerbates the problem of the imagination. For, a figurative synthesis has the character of spontaneity, and this determinative capacity eludes mere receptivity. This synthesis, even as it finds itself confined within the horizons of transcendental apperception, exceeds the limits of sensibility, which is after all, as suggested in our reading of the A Deduction, one of the necessary conditions for any possible mediation between sensibility and understanding.

Yet, just as soon as we seem to detect a continuity in the treatment of the imagination, as a transcendental imagination, even if one that must be 'incarcerated' within the disciplinary unity of apperception, Kant confronts us with more difficulty: 'This synthesis is an action of the understanding on the sensibility; and is its first application – and thereby the ground of all its other applications – to the objects of our possible intuition' (NKS 165; B152). The figurative synthesis differs from that of the intellectual in the inclusion of the imagination in its operation. But, since the imagination can be included in this *a priori* synthesis, Kant calls it *productive*. This inclusion, of course, is due to the direction from, and hence its relation to, apperception. Thus, a productive capacity of imagination is only possible due to the connection of the latter with apperception. Or, the containment itself is the true source and reality of a transcendental imagination, and thus, the autonomous (from *scientific* consciousness) creative imagination becomes at best, a mere myth, at worst, an occult enthusiasm. The reproductive imagination, having played such an important role in the A Deduction, even deemed in a certain sense as transcendental, is cast away into the contingent domain of psychological research.

But, what is most remarkable is Kant's characterisation of the intellectual synthesis as that which 'is carried out by the understanding alone, without the aid of imagination' (NKS 163; B152). This depiction forces us to ask a very simple question: Is such a synthesis possible by the understanding – alone? For after all, each and every synthesis is the 'mere product of the power of imagination. . .' (NKS 111; A78, B103). Moreover, what has happened to the characterisation of transcendental logic in which a 'pure synthesis of representations' is brought to the concept? (NKS 112; A78–79, B104). These examples, in A and B, tell quite a different story from the figurative synthesis, which is merely 'an action of understanding on the sensibility'. There is, of course, the allusion to the participation of imagination, but it is merely a conduit of access to sensibility, and no longer exhibits the status of the A Deduction.[18] This seems to be possible due to some 'innate' power of understanding to perform synthetic acts, an exclusive power that is nowhere demonstrated.

It is in this context that Kant alludes to the paradox which surrounds the distinction of appearance and thing in itself. As we have already encountered, this distinction, and the confinement of our knowledge to the former is required if there is to be knowledge with the character of necessity and universality. However, and this is where the paradox re-emerges into the light, Kant writes: 'we intuit ourselves only as we are inwardly *affected*, and this would seem to be contradictory, since we should then have to be in a passive relation [of active affection] to ourselves' (NKS 166; B153). Or, in other words, the self, as it is grounded upon the unity of apperception, must also be in some sense a non-unity, as activity and passivity, spontaneity and receptivity. It is these stems which must be brought together into a mediating relation in such a way that spontaneity, and therefore, transcendental unity, remains the highest principle. Yet, Kant achieves this unity, and removes the paradox in a questionable fashion (much as Fichte will do in the next generation). He reiterates that it is the understanding which has an '. . .original power of combining the manifold', the product of which it brings 'under an apperception'. (NKS 166; B153)

However, the understanding is not a faculty of intuitions, neither intellectual, nor sensible. In the figurative synthesis, it required imagination, i.e., a synthesis, which it contained in itself. Thus, what Kant is calling an intellectual synthesis is one allegedly performed by the understanding; but it acts neither on intuition (figurative), nor upon concepts themselves, for this would contradict the project of a critique of pure reason. Kant specifies the synthesis of the pure understanding, or reason:

> Its synthesis, therefore, if the synthesis be viewed by itself alone, is nothing but the unity of the act, of which, as an act, it is conscious to itself, even without [the aid of] sensibility, but through which it is yet able to determine the sensibility. (NKS 166; B153)

This pure *a priori* unity of the act of apperception, as pure spontaneity, assures that the understanding and its concepts can determine 'sensibility inwardly' (NKS 166; B153). Significantly, Kant writes, attempting poorly to come to terms with imagination:

> Thus the understanding, under the title of a *transcendental synthesis of imagination*, performs this act upon the *passive* subject, whose *faculty* it is, and we are therefore justified in saying that inner sense is affected thereby. Apperception and its synthetic unity is . . . very far from being identical with inner sense. (NKS 166; B153–54)

Kant gives to the imagination now only a title of that which mediates inner sense and apperception, and which allows him to resolve the paradox of a 'passive relation of active affection' to oneself. For, imagination is in the background of this entire paradox.

Inner sense, or time, holds within itself the structure of the imagination as at once the (spontaneous) form of pure intuition and the receptivity of the passive relation. Moreover, it must be run through and held together in a figurative synthesis, as in the reproductive imagination, in order for there to be any determinate intuition. Yet, that which is given pre-eminence is the unity of apperception and its consciousness of this figurative synthesis (and the directorial credit for the action of combination itself and for the production of the manifold in its affection of sense).

In each of these references to the revisions of the B Edition, it can be ascertained that synthesis is being taken over from the imagination, but the transformation is rather messy, as Kant seems to be making every effort to diminish any notion of an imaginative capacity which is not actually the work of the understanding. It is either a *title* for a particular act of the imagination, or it is the understanding itself either producing the manifold of appearance, or acting upon inner sense. Yet, he once desperately needed the imagination in order to establish the unity of knowledge. In any event, it must be admitted that there has been a radical shift in the status of imagination, to the extent that there is a real question of its existence as a faculty at all.

In the A Deduction, where imagination was a presupposition of apperception, and thus, of the understanding, it is implied that the understanding would be presented with objects assembled for itself from the synthesis of imagination, and that it was the role of the concept to recognise the outcome. In other words, and even though apperception incites and gives logical unity to the endeavour, and hence a determinate connection, a proper knowledge, the imagination still had control over its own sphere of operations, as with differing artisans upon the floor, and not yet as various 'appendages to the machine' with respect to the totality of consciousness. Since imagination has an immediate contact with intuition, it gives rise to a type of 'knowledge', which, while not necessary in any strict sense, sets forth a pre-experiential awareness of our being in the world. What has changed between the two Deductions is therefore more than a mere change in presentation. If the unity of apperception must be the alpha and omega of pure, *a priori* knowledge, then it would seem that the imagination would be somewhere in between, in either edition. Yet, the status of the imagination would differ, as we have seen, depending on whether it were a presupposition of apperception in a genealogy of synthetic knowledge, or if it were contained in apperception, and to that extent only its name, as a formal indicator, remained, as it is absorbed in the 'cybernetic loop' of a single, unchangeable and total consciousness.

As Kant claimed in his discussion of Leibniz and Wolff, the synthesis of imagination is not only necessary, but can, without logical or conceptual accompaniment build an empirical knowledge, which, while not ultimately necessary, persists as the modality of inductive and inventive terrestrial knowledge. Such a space of non-logical, non-conceptual 'knowledge' seemed assured by the A edition, which emphasised the imagination as a third basic faculty of the soul. But, the scenario of a transcendental unity of consciousness, of an original unity of apperception, seems to suggest that, while we may speculate as to the existence of a non-logical world, one that is not related to apperception, there is emphatically no outside, and there is nothing that can be represented, be known, if it is not brought before consciousness.

As Kant commanded, all combination, 'be we conscious of it or not', is the mere result of the understanding, and this is assured by the absorption of imagination into the apperception. And in this way, its pure act could be deemed a synthesis, but only if the imagination is contained within the understanding, or, as a modality of consciousness. It is still left to be decided whether or not this usurpation has any legitimacy, which is another way of stating the paradox.

Study questions

1. What is the purpose of the Transcendental Deduction? Why is it necessary? Is Kant's argument convincing?
2. Is there a difference between the First and Second Edition Transcendental Deductions? If so, what is the difference or are the differences?

TRANSCENDENTAL JUDGMENT: JUDGMENT AND SCHEMATISM
(NKS 177; A132/B171)

The principles of pure understanding are generated through the 'mother-wit' of transcendental judgment, which Kant describes as a 'faculty of subsuming under rules' (A132, B172). That which is subsumed *under concepts* is the manifold of appearance; sensibility is given rules via judgment. In this way, it is judgment which is the mediating bridge between sensibility and understanding. Or, as it was formulated in the B Deduction, transcendental judgment is a synthetic action of understanding upon sensibility. In the A Deduction, this transcendental judgment would occur via a synthesis of representations and of its recognition by the concept. In both cases, the implication is that the imagination, whether it is the presupposition of apperception, or is contained therein, brings the stems or sources of knowledge together into a synthetic experience. However, what is meant by the claim that it is the imagination that is somehow responsible for judgment? Is this not the jurisdiction of logic – or does this point to the need for an *a priori* imagination? As we have already seen, Kant unfolds a distinction within logic, that between general and transcendental logics. He reminds us that the former exhibits the pure forms and faculties of thought, abstracted from all content, alone unto itself. Or, as he suggests toward the end of the work, general logic is a 'canon for understanding and reason in general. . .' (NKS 630; A796, B825). Transcendental logic, on the contrary, must be involved with a 'certain content', or, as in A, a synthesis of representations, if, that is, there is to be any knowledge. Again, we are not concerned therefore with general logic in that we are seeking synthetic *a priori* knowledge of the manifold of objects of appearance.[19]

Transcendental logic shows us our capacity to found an *a priori* knowledge which extends beyond merely analytic criteria of truth or of a dialectical logic of illusion, the antinomial matrix of the non-objective inferences of reason. And, as we have seen, that which distinguishes transcendental from formal logic is thus the involvement of the synthesis of imagination as a necessary condition for the fabrication of experience and knowledge.

But, what type of involvement does the imagination have in this practice of transcendental judgment? And, can the contours of this involvement shed light on the previous question of the treatment of the imagination in the two Deductions? Moreover, in an attempt to answer the previous question, since Kant has implied that judgment in this way is distinct from understanding, does this imply that transcendental judgment, as the application of empty concepts to a manifold of appearance *in concreto* is an operation of imagination, which thus has a distinct status with respect to the understanding? And, does this not further imply that understanding, as a faculty of mere rules is utterly dependent upon a power which straddles the vast ditch which separates understanding from sensibility? Is this natural gift of judgment, to which Kant alludes, distinct from the empty recitation of rules by the understanding, and does it not depend upon creativity, which cannot be learned, but only allowed to act? As we will see, transcendental judgment, as in the Schematism, is such an art of bringing together that which exists now only as the severed stems of knowledge. Kant describes the purpose of transcendental philosophy with respect to these questions:

It must formulate by means of universal but sufficient marks the conditions under which objects can be given in harmony with these concepts. Otherwise the concepts would be void of all content, and therefore mere logical forms, not pure concepts of the understanding. (NKS 179; A136, B175)

The objects are to be given in harmony with pure concepts by means of 'universal and sufficient marks', which facilitate the fulfilment of the concept in the intuition. In this context, judgment indicates a cultivation of harmony between the object and the concept in order for these to be given together as a unified experience. We can fathom from the terms 'marks' that there is to be a bridge between the universal and the particular by means of the 'marking' judgment. But what is this judgment if it is not the logical function of judgment discussed earlier? In order to answer this and the other questions which have been raised, we will turn to 'Schematism of the Pure Concepts of Understanding', a section which became central to Heidegger in his interpretation of the significance of the revisions in *Kant and the Problem of Metaphysics*. This will be followed by a sketch of the Principles of Pure Understanding, which Kant declares to be synthetic *a priori* judgments proper, the main goal of his inquiry.

Study questions

1. What is the meaning of transcendental judgment and why is it necessary?
2. What is the relationship between transcendental judgment and time?

The Schematism of Pure Concepts (NKS 180; A137/B176)

Kant introduces his discussion of schematism by reminding his reader of the purpose and the procedure of transcendental judgment, i.e., the 'subsumption' of an object under a concept. A subsumption, as it implies a 'contact' between heterogeneous poles, sensibility and understanding, requires that there is some homogeneity which would serve as a 'conduit' for the subsumption.[20] Recalling his designation of the imagination as the mediating power between sensibility and understanding at A124, Kant writes:

Obviously there must be some third thing, which is homogeneous on the one hand with the category, and on the other hand with the appearance, and which thus makes the application of the former to the latter possible. This mediating representation must be pure, that is, void of all empirical content, and yet at the same time, while it must in one respect be *intellectual* it must in another be *sensible*. (NKS 181; A138, B178)

The representation which fulfils the criteria for the mediation is the transcendental schema, which as a transcendental determination of time (the formal condition of inner sense), provides the conduit for an 'indirect' meeting of the category and appearance. A schema is homogeneous with the category in that it provides the unity which is required for there is to be a singular temporality. Further, it is homogeneous with appearance since 'time is contained in every empirical representation of the manifold' (NKS 181; A139, B178). It is thus the schema which, as a necessary third thing, is solely responsible for the application of the category to appearance. And, Kant declares, once again raising many questions, the schema is 'always a product of the imagination' (NKS 182; A140, B179).[21]

Kant asserts that this schema, while not equivalent to either the category or to the manifold of appearance, is somehow contained by the concept, as an *a priori* and formal condition of sensibility (inner sense). What this seems to imply is that the schema must operate at the behest of the category, in the sense of a schema *of the concept*. Such a requirement, as we have seen in our previous reading, is extant in both Deductions in greater or lesser extents. However, it remains difficult to grasp how such a mediation is possible if the mediating schema is contained by the concept.

This notion of containment seems to be a distinct claim to that involved in the distinction between an image and a schema, where the latter must act in accordance with the directives of apperceptive unity, while the former need not act in accord with this unity. What this suggests is that the schema is the product of imagination which is orchestrated for the understanding, even if it remains possible to consider its other operations. Moreover, if apperception contains the synthesis, how is it to obtain a mediate relationship with time? If it contained this synthesis, and if the schema was produced by this synthesis by means of a relationship of determination vis-à-vis temporality, would not apperception have in its own heart the anxiety of its own finitude?

What is still at stake in Kant's recasting of the Deduction is the meaning of an *a priori* containment of the formal conditions of sensibility, and of the power of synthesis, within the concept. Is such a notion compatible with the workings of schematism? Or is this notion of containment merely a cognitive principle, setting forth the requirement of an 'I think' beside every representation? Yet, such a notion of containment is not the same as that which is operative in the B Deduction, for in the latter, there is not only the cognitive requirement of an 'I think', but the productive claim of 'I make, I synthesise'. For the understanding *is* imagination in so far as the former is, in B, a synthetic power. Indeed, one is tempted to conclude that the term imagination is maintained only for the sake of custom. As a strong contrast, Kant writes in his description of the schematism:

> This schematism of our understanding, in its application to appearances and their mere form, is an art concealed in the depths of the human soul, whose real modes of activity nature is hardly likely ever to allow us to discover, and have open to our gaze. (NKS 183; A141, B180–81)

It would be hasty to dismiss such a description as mere poetising on the part of Kant, for it suggests that there is a dimension of the activity of the power of imagination which (as he has intimated before) remains concealed from the gaze of the understanding, or, in other words, that the truth of the works of the power of transcendental imagination are inaccessible, and distinct from, the domain of consciousness.

Such poetical language suggests that Kant has been confronted with the limits of expression, limits which symptomatise limits in access to the totality of relevant experience. Such limitations, or better, the realisation of such limits, throw the previously unproblematic presupposition regarding the unity of apperception into serious question. In such a case, if the orchestrations of the imagination must remain hidden from the gaze of consciousness, and are the presuppositions of this consciousness, are we not obliged to consider the question of unity unanswered? Does not such an assertion of unity transcend the limits of experience, if, that is, we cannot verify such a claim of unity since the relevant data must remain hidden from our conscious surveillance?

However, Kant does not question the unity of apperception, and in his presupposing of this unity, specifies the 'third thing' that will allow for his apperceptive unity to ultimately rule a manifold of appearance. This 'third thing' is necessary since a mere image, as a product of the reproductive imagination, as with an accidental collocation, cannot be congruent with the concept. Thus, a schema, the product of the productive imagination, may be congruent with the concept in that it cannot be brought into an image. It is a monogram of the pure *a priori* imagination, however, which Kant will still regard as in need of a concept, and thus, pure synthesis itself may be deployed by the concept in accordance with its directives of unity.[22] He defines the schema as a

> product which concerns the determination of inner sense in general according to conditions of its form (time), in respect of all representations, so far as the representations are to be connected *a priori* in one concept in conformity with the unity of apperception. (NKS 183; A142, B181)

In the foregoing, Kant seems to uphold on the one hand the *principal* distinction of pure *a priori* imagination and understanding. This is amplified by his echoes of his earlier enigmatic language with respect to an 'art concealed in the depths of the human soul', an art which will remained concealed from our gaze. Such language, in its acknowledgement of the limits of human understanding, seems to be out of tune with that of the B Deduction in its assertion of the total reach of conceptual unity, 'be we conscious of it or not'. Such an assertion, together with the rather forced identification of the transcendental imagination with the understanding, as a mere title of an act of understanding, seems to be out of step with the intrinsic constitution of human knowledge and of its conditions of possibility. Yet, this does not excuse the imagination from compliance with the directives of unity, but raises other questions with respect to the relation of temporality and consciousness. That which is raised also is the possibility of other truths, ones, as with practical reason, which are beyond the horizons of the theoretical project.[23]

However, even if imagination must act in accord with the unity of apperception (if we are to preserve the intrinsic meaning of the Kantian *a priori*), the significance and role of imagination is so vast that it must remain a central feature of our study of all aspects of the Critical Philosophy. Kant elaborates this centrality through a determination of the object of the schematism. After listing the schema for each of the concepts of understanding, he informs us that the schema 'contains and makes capable of representation only a determination of time' (NKS 185; A145, B184), that they are

> . . . nothing but *a priori* determinations of time in accordance with rules. These rules relate in the order of the categories to the *time-series*, the *time-content*, the *time-order*, and lastly to the *scope of time* in respect of all possible objects. (NKS 185; A145, B184–85)

It is in this way, that, in conjunction with the categories and intuition, the pure, *a priori* power of imagination generates the nexus of temporality. To this extent, alone, it is the mediating bridge between the antitheses of understanding and sensibility. It is by means of its capacity for direct contact with the manifold of intuition that imagination provides the preconditions for an indirect correspondence between apperception (spontaneity) and the pure intuition of inner sense (receptivity). In the absence of schemata, which realise and restrict the concepts, the latter have a merely logical meaning, as the 'functions of the understanding for concepts; and represent no objects' (NKS 187; A147, B187). It would seem that such a schematic power of realisation and restriction of the concept would confirm the vital independence of imagination.[24] How else is apperception to have at least a theoretical distance from temporality?

Study questions

1. Why is a schematism necessary in light of the Kantian project? Does Kant's treatment of imagination in this section come into conflict with his revisions of the Second Edition?
2. Would it be possible, as Heidegger suggests, to regard the schematism as the source of the pure concepts? What would that mean for the Kantian project?

THE PRINCIPLES OF PURE UNDERSTANDING (NKS 188; A148/B187)

The principles are those transcendental judgments which are achieved *a priori* by a synthesis of imagination, the activity of which has been subsumed under a rule-matrix of an understanding. More precisely, the system of principles catalogues the variation of conceptual subsumptions of the syntheses of imagination, via a fourfold specification of the schemata, as the Axioms, Anticipations, Analogies, and Postulates. This fourfold specification is itself divided between two respective classes regarding their respective natures of certainty, whether immediate and intuitive, i.e., mathematical, or mediate and discursive, i.e., dynamical. Kant writes:

> The principles of pure understanding, whether constitutive *a priori*, like the mathematical principles or merely regulative, like the dynamical, contain nothing but what may be called the pure schema of possible experience. (NKS 258; A236–237, B296)

This schema, a transcendental determination of time, is a work of the imagination, according to the directives of apperception. In other words, the schema of imagination allows a representation to be given to consciousness of time, which otherwise cannot be an object of possible intuition. The schema is the possibility of a 'third thing' which can serve as the locus of mediation between the stems or sources, understanding and sensibility. Or, schema allow for there to be a relation between apperception and time, of the unity of the concept and the forms of inner sense.

Schemata, as the principles of the pure understanding, are thus purported to be the answer to the original question proposed by Kant: how are synthetic *a priori* judgments possible? And, since this question is the same as that which asks after the possibility of a unity of experience in general, Kant unifies the four principles by the assertion of a highest principle of synthetic judgment: 'Every object stands under the necessary condition of synthetic unity of the manifold of intuition in a possible experience' (NKS 194; A158, B197). Unity, in this sense, is thus the highest schema of pure experience.

This bald assertion of unity of the concept is, however, limited by its embeddedness amidst the horizons of possible experience, as in their status as synthetic, and not analytic, judgments, there must be a consideration of 'content' as a condition of possibility of experience as such. Yet, this limitation purportedly allows the understanding to know with complete, *a priori* certainty the realm of phenomena, since the manifold of appearance is a construction of its own spontaneous and synthetic consciousness. It knows what it has placed there itself. In this island of truth, we would be, for Kant, certain of a unity between the concept and intuition, by means of the schema of imagination. This is not a question of knowledge of any things themselves, if we are to construct the conditions for *a priori* knowledge in the Kantian sense. The mediation concerns representations, and is a synthesis of representations. And, by reflective inference, the mediation is the unification of the faculties of the soul, or in other words, the subsumption of the imagination under the unity of the concept of understanding, and a subsumption of imagination in its *a priori*, transcendental sense under the Ideal of Reason. It is this drive to unity in consciousness which answers the question of the possibility of synthetic *a priori* judgments. Kant writes:

> Synthetic *a priori* judgments are thus possible when we relate the formal conditions of *a priori* intuition, the synthesis of imagination and the necessary unity of this synthesis in a transcendental apperception, to a possible empirical knowledge in general. We then assert that the conditions of the *possibility of experience* in general are likewise conditions of the *possibility of the object of experience*, and that for this reason, they have objective validity in a synthetic *a priori* judgment. (NKS 194; A158, B197)

The *conditions for the possibility of experience* are the *conditions for the objects of experience* – or, synthetic *a priori* judgments are possible if the *a priori* conditions are capable of coming together into a unity which could ground a *possible experience* in general.

Kant proceeds to show in each principle of the pure understanding in what sense the imagination is subsumed under the matrix of unity. Indeed, the operations of subsumption which give rise to the principles, is, with the schematism, precisely this deployment of the imagination according to the conceptual parameters in play.

For instance, in the Axioms of Intuition, extensive magnitudes arise from the 'successive synthesis of the productive imagination in the generation of figures' (NKS 199; A163, B204). This power of synthesis is simply the power of adding part to part, but, as Kant asserts, the imagination can do many things, but it can never decide: which one? It is only the unity of the concept which can decide. Kant writes:

> If I assert that through three lines, two of which taken together are greater than the third, a triangle can be described, I have expressed merely the function of productive imagination whereby

the lines meet at any and every possible angle. (NKS 200; A164–65, B205)

The undecidability of the blind imagination, is due, for Kant, to the absence from the works of imagination of a specific type of unity, one that is the condition of necessary and universal connections between representations. Once again, imagination, by itself, can never generate an *a priori* knowledge (although it may itself operate in accordance with another notion of the *a priori*), even though it possesses transcendental status either by nature (A Deduction), or by mere association with the unity of apperception (B Deduction).

In a note to the Axioms added in the B Edition, Kant makes a distinction between composition and connection, the former having no necessary connection, recalling the collocative framing in the Aesthetic, the latter having constituents that 'necessarily belong to one another, as . . . the accident to some substance, or the effect to the cause' (NKS 198; B201). Although it might appear unjustified that the concept would subsume the synthesis of representations under its conditions of unity, the discussion in the Axioms deems the imagination to be indecisive, a charge which Kant wants to make stick, for it allows him to win his argument via other means. For, if this charge were in fact true, the synthesis of imagination would need, if there was to be a determinate yet pure knowledge, the unity of the concept due to its own lack of capacity, incompleteness, blindness.

We will find that in each of the principles, the strategy is to characterise the imagination and its synthesis as in some manner deficient, or insufficient, to the requirements of *a priori* knowledge. Therefore, with the next principle, the Anticipations of Perception, even though the imaginative synthesis is the faculty of instantaneous apprehension, the moment of vision, since it occurs via the 'repetition of an ever-ceasing synthesis', apprehends, *a posteriori*, a continuity of intermediate sensations, possible realities. Thus, imagination is essentially *a posteriori* and discontinuous. This lack of continuity, of course, leads to the association of the imagination with the unity of apperception.

Similarly, in the Analogies of Experience, the imagination orchestrates a threefold synthesis, each synthesis corresponding to a modality of temporality in its relationships with the composition of a manifold of appearance (duration, succession, and co-existence).

What is at stake is a 'necessary connection' of perceptions. This principle demands that the unity of apperception is projected as the seat of the alleged unity of time, as a subjectum of inner experience. To recall the distinction made in the A Deduction between connection (synthesis) and determinate connection (recognition), imagination is not capable of making a necessary connection, and once again, must submit to the concept, if appearance is to be subsumed under a concept via a schema of merely possible experience.

Each of the aspects of time have an analogy, or a schema that allows it a conscious representation, respectively: substance, as a surrogate for a hidden time, a regulative ground of permanency as against the ever-ceasing synthesis of imagination. Moreover, in the Analogy of Succession, the imagination connects a past with the present in a synthesis, for example, in the figure:

$$A \text{\textemdash\textemdash\textemdash} B$$

However, Kant informs us that the imagination can make either of the two successive times the first or last, and vice versa. It once again possesses no rule by which it may decide which one is first and which is last. It thus has no rule to confer objective validity, proper order and necessary connection. It is in this light that Kant explains the seeming mystery of objectivity: 'We can extract clear concepts of them from experience, only because we have put them into experience, and . . . experience is thus itself brought about only by their means' (NKS 223; A196, B 241). Furthermore, the Third Analogy, that of co-existence, or principle of reciprocity, closely resembles the back and forth play of the power of imagination. However, once again, Kant asserts that the imagination cannot hold these two representations together with a necessary connection, and therefore, that a rule would be needed which would claim that the ground or condition of each was in the other, in other words, as a community. Kant gives a summary of the Analogies, which provides a description of temporalisation as such, as a synthesis according to rules, when he writes:

> Our Analogies portray the unity of nature in the connection of all appearances under certain exponents which express nothing save the relation of time (in so far as time comprehends all existence) to the unity of apperception – such unity being possible only in synthesis according to rules. (NKS 237; A216, B 263)

But, in this passage, we are given the reason why the concept has its association with the imagination, since not only can this power give a coherent content for the actualisation of this unity, it can also allow for a mediate relationship between the spontaneous act of apperception and the receptive affectation of sensibility. Once again, and especially with the usage of the phrase a 'third thing', this raises the question of the status of imagination.

In the Postulates of Empirical Knowledge, the mantra that the works of imagination have no necessity is delineated in more detail, from possibility to actuality, and then to necessity. The possible is anything that is in agreement with the formal conditions of experience, concepts and intuitions. The actual is bound up with material conditions, with sensation. Necessity is the actual in agreement with the universal conditions of experience. With regard to the Postulate of Possibility, the imagination is painted as a mere dreamer, thinking possibility after possibility, just as long as its works are not monsters which violate the law of contradiction. Within these logical horizons, therefore, the power of imagination and its 'natural' relationship to possibility is harnessed for its synthetic activity 'in relation to experience, and within its limits' (NKS 242; A224, B271).

The Postulate of Actuality, or existence, is possible without perception; it can be known, or suspected by means of inference, for example. The role of content for the concept is that it provides the mark of actuality. In this attempt to glance at this mark, Kant adds in B a 'Refutation of Idealism', a charge which was made of the *Critique* by many contemporaries, especially Schulze.[25] In this refutation, imagination becomes the culprit of idealism, the idea that our experience is merely illusion, imaginary. In a specific way, Kant seems to be distancing himself from the perceptive imagination in a note in the A Deduction in which he states that imagination is involved in perception. Indeed, the criterion for a refutation of idealism becomes to 'show that we have *experience*, and not merely a mere imagination of outer things' (NKS 244; B275). The question of objects 'outside us' becomes the question of an 'outer sense', distinct from an 'outer imagination' (NKS 246; B277). Thus, Kant thought that he had to rebuke the power of imagination in order to escape the charge of solipsism and/or subjective idealism.

Finally, with respect to the Postulate of Necessity, Kant writes that without the hypothetical necessity of subsumption under concepts, laws, etc., there could be no 'nature'. This latter is fully articulated via a nexus of laws. Kant, in a direct echo of his earlier characterisation of imagination as blind, writes that no necessity in nature is blind, which of course is a restatement of the highest principle of synthetic *a priori* judgments, stated in different terms, that time must stand under the necessary unity of apperception. It is the nexus of the concept which projects unity upon the accidental compositions and rhapsodies of imagination.

Study questions

1. Given Kant's sustained criticism of the concept of substance, how is this latter notion to be regarded and used within Kant's Critical Philosophy?
2. How are each of the principles of pure reason constituted through the subsumption of the imagination under a concept?

BLINDNESSES: THE STATUS OF IMAGINATION IN THE FIRST *CRITIQUE*

It would be difficult to deny that the imagination would not hold up that well within the parameters of the Kantian criteria of *a priori* knowledge, as this latter is determined, ultimately, by the unity of theoretical reason, the understanding. However, even if the true meaning of the possibility of synthetic *a priori* judgments is in fact the possibility of a legitimate subsumption of the imagination under the unity of the concept, there would still be flexibility with respect to the means by which such a subsumption was performed. For instance, in the A Deduction, it seemed that the imagination was in fact autonomous, except when it was required by the unity of apperception in order to construct a particular *a priori* judgment. In this light, there would be a wider notion of consciousness, or in other words, the awareness of waking life, without the necessity of a limited, apodeictic consciousness, surveilling each and every contour of this awareness. However, such is the main implication of the B Deduction, that every representation, 'be we conscious of it or not', is subject to the unity of apperception. This is why an a-logical, a-conceptual world is that of myth.

However, another question could be asked: can the requirements of apodeictic certainty truly be met in a situation in which there is, as in the A Deduction, an imagination that is presupposed as a condition of possibility for the unity of apperception? Could the

a priori of the *Critique* be satisfied if it were possible that the understanding and its concepts resulted from autonomous syntheses
of the imagination? For, even if Kant incessantly seeks to lower
the status of imagination, and thereby emphasise its need of the
concept, he is still forced to acknowledge, with qualifications, the significance of imagination. For example, Kant writes with respect to
the unconditioned itself:

> This unconditioned is always contained in *the absolute totality of
> the series* as represented in imagination. But this absolutely com-
> plete synthesis is again only an idea; for we cannot know, at least
> at the start of this enquiry, whether such a synthesis is possible in
> the case of appearance. (NKS 391; A416, B444)

Once again, we see that the transcendental imagination has a power
to potentially synthesise the absolute series of conditions, and it
thereby allows for the ideal projection of a totality which contains the
idea of the unconditioned – which is an Idea of Reason, as we will
see below in the Transcendental Dialectic. It seems only to be its relations with time that keep it from attaining its goal. Yet, the goal of
totality is not that of imagination, but of reason. The former, because
of its relationship with time, because of its being as time, forbids it
true access to reason: it fashions the ideal but has no comprehension
of it, and no ideal of its own. Since the imagination fails in this way,
in Kant's eyes, it thereby loses its right to independence; it is deemed
by reason and its tribunal, 'Guilty!', sentenced to an indefinite period
of hard labour without ever comprehending its alleged crime.

The revisions made between the two editions must not be simply
interpreted as Kant attempting to achieve a better clarity of expression. What is at stake in these revisions exceeds the question of the
conditions of possibility for an *a priori* knowledge. For, as we have
seen above, the imagination participates in the constitution of *a
priori* knowledge, but in two mutually exclusive ways. In itself as a
presupposition of the event of apperception, or, as contained within
the web of apperception. Kant is not seeking merely *a priori* knowledge, but a specific form of *a priori* knowledge, which, as we can see
from his decision for the latter in the B Deduction, has for its alpha
and omega the command and control of experience by reason.

In light of the diminishment of the imagination, the excision of
A94–95 need not only be read as a desire on the part of Kant to

remove the appearance of a physiological genealogy, an appearance due to the 'random groping' of the A Deduction. For it could be ventured to suggest that instead of Locke and Hume, Kant may have well written of Hamann and Jacobi or other champions of empiricism and imagination, such as the anarchist writer, Heinse, as 'enthusiasts', each and every one, as Kant names them. Kant borrows the term from Hume, himself at odds with reason, but deploys it against those philosophies, such as Hamann's, which bore the greatest resemblance to Hume's.[26] For it is not merely empiricism and the source of the concepts which is at stake. Instead, that which is at stake is the authority of reason in its practical deployment. We will defer this discussion to the chapter below on the Receptions and Influence.

In the next section, I will continue on in our reading of the First *Critique* with an exploration of the grand distinction between the phenomena and noumena, of the web of representation organised by the principle of sufficient reason and the super-sensible, or intelligible, dimension of which we can have no knowledge. We will ascertain that there is another type of 'knowing' which is that of practical reason. In this way, there exists for consciousness two ways to know which are simultaneous, two ways to regard the world as it discloses itself to us. Alongside of our theoretical construction of the phenomena, there are the truths, precepts and imperatives of practical reason which describe the existence of the noumenal realm, to which the theoretical must remain blind, just as reason must remain blind to (or at least untouched by) the domain of the empirical.

Study questions

1. What were the main issues and who were the major disputants of the 'pantheism controversy'? Was Kant correct to come down on the side of the rationalists and the authority of reason?
2. Is philosophy possible without the authority of reason? Can we conceive of a non-rational philosophy that is still philosophy?

PHENOMENA AND NOUMENA (NKS 257; A235/B294)

We have explored in the preceding sections an array of answers to the question, 'How are synthetic *a priori* judgments possible?' The answers that we have found moreover are each aspects of the grand construction of the architectonic of knowledge with the character of necessity and universality. In the following, I would like to illustrate the complexity of the phenomena, retracing our steps on the way to an understanding of the labyrinth of representational consciousness. I will next consider the implications for such a consciousness in light of the dependence of representation upon the original presence of the 'thing-in-itself' (*Ding an sich*). This original presence intimates the dimension of the noumena, an ultimate referent, or as we have seen, transcendental object. But, we can only 'think' it, and describe it in negations. It is in action and ethical judgment, as we will see in the Second *Critique*, that we can have immediate access to the noumena. For Kant, the noumenal dimension is the transcendental ground for freedom, it is that which transcends the labyrinth of theoretical reason into a practical domain which 'makes room for faith'.

We begin in the first *Critique* with an immediate recognition of the unity of experience. It only seems that practical existence among mortals does not necessarily fit into this grand *mathesis* of unity and order. But, in its own realm, theoretical reason is held captive by the image of its own unity. It begins with the fact of experience and then asks, 'How is this possible?' It conducts an analysis of the transcendental conditions of possibility for an experience which it grants the character of unity. That is to say, the presupposition of unity merely testifies to the contention that the world is intelligible. Yet, as this intelligibility is projected from an active consciousness, it becomes necessary to locate the organisational principles of experience in consciousness itself. Such an insight into the status of objects as representations of consciousness is in fact the emergence of self-consciousness. From the perspective of transcendental idealism, a phenomenological investigation into the phenomenon is actually a self-examination of reason in its various comportments amidst existence. In this way, being is grounded in thought and this thought, as reason, has various dimensions and aspects in a way that is *isomorphic* with the nexus of the phenomenon. Indeed, the phenomenon is merely consciousness in its theoretical posture – consciousness, reason itself, is merely a stand-in for the *logos*, language, which expresses and determines it, as Hamann held. Yet, as Kant was seeking to defend the authority of reason, he could not countenance the near Wittgensteinian anarchy of language and its games. Reason is not just another language game for Kant, it is the master of the games, of the various dimensions of its care.

The phenomenon, as we have seen, has been shown to be a quite complex 'thing'. We begin in the labyrinth of representations, forever scratching the surface, able, like the prisoners in Plato's cave, only to sketch the relations amidst the representations, pictures that captivate us. Some event initially frees us from the worst chains, and we take a step back in order to explore the meaning of existence. One aspect of this meaning is the theoretical determination, but there are other still unexplored regions. We witness the experience, and then we analyse it into space, time and myriad concepts. The First *Critique* in essence gives merely the results of Kant's own explorations in thought. It is the very possibility of a free act of thought itself which gives body and life to the architectonic of reason. But, this submerged ground in *praxis*, intimated by thought, calls us to begin to approach the transcendental condition for the phenomenon itself, and thus, to apprehend the noumena in practical existence.

The phenomenon is described by Kant as the consciousness, and thus, self-consciousness, of the grand projections of the pure intuitions of space and time and of the pure concepts in their synthetic union in the apperceptive (imagination). For us, as Kant says, there is only representation. Yet, there persists the question of the outside or perhaps the inside of the phenomenon. He acknowledges this question with his own designation of the transcendental object = 'X'.

That which is essential is that, for him, the noumena is not to be considered 'metaphysically' – or better, substantively. The *new* metaphysics is seeking to criticise the 'mere play of concepts', each of which transcends the horizon of possible experience. Under the spell of Hume, Kant regards sensibility or intuition in a merely empirical manner. Moreover, as all sensibility becomes entangled in the nexus of representation, there can be no privileged feelings that could evade determination as representations, unlike Schopenhauer who held that pleasure and pain directly intimate the in-itself of the world. This is not Kant's ambition. However, it could be asked, especially in light of his later insights in the Third *Critique*, if a differing way of seeing could have indeed been possible within the Kantian notion of intuition. This question is specially relevant with respect to the development of German Idealism, within which the act of *intellectual intuition* was its primary theoretical characteristic. The latter notion became the cornerstone in a system of pure reason as the fountain for the disclosure of truth. As it was immediately evident as a state of self-consciousness, there was no need to prove it. But, Kant's endeavours remain critical and his division of the domains of reason never achieves unity. It could indeed be questioned if a critical philosophy could ever be developed in the context of a unified system.

Despite the initially Humean conception of intuition in the *Critique of Pure Reason*, Kant does offer us an explicit manner by which we can, even amidst the world as representation, gain insight into the explicit possibility of another dimension beyond the domain of theoretical reason. Such a disclosure takes place in the Transcendental Dialectic, to which we now turn. However, as we will see, many of the analyses across the following pages of the First *Critique* are in many ways an echo of Kant's *Inaugural Dissertation*, which sought to clearly distinguish the sensible from the intelligible realm, the empirical from the understanding. We have already had an intimation of this with the distinction between the phenomenon and noumena. The fundamental significance of this distinction will play itself out in the Paralogisms, Antinomies and the Ideal.

Yet, before we turn to the Transcendental Dialectic *per se*, we will examine another variation of the differentiation of the sensible from the intelligible with a consideration of the Kantian Amphiboly. It will be with this notion that Kant will be able to carry through the rest of his criticism of pure reason *and* pure empiricism.

The Amphiboly of Concepts of Reflection (NKS 276; A260/B316)

Perhaps the most visible traces of the *Inaugural Dissertation* are found in the section on the *amphibolous* use of language and concepts in illegitimate ways. Indeed, it is this section which introduces a criterion for judgments with regard to the proper jurisdiction of concepts vis-à-vis the phenomenal and noumenal *topoi* (places, or, as Kant suggests, its *transcendental location*). The integrity of the critical architectonic rests upon this capacity of the assignment of jurisdiction with respect to the varying array of concepts, and of their differing origins. Some of Kant's heirs, such as Carnap, use this notion of amphiboly in a markedly different sense from Kant, and we should be aware of this *logical positivist* reading which sought to construct an ideal language free of logical and empirical ambiguity, even if this meant eliminating any notion of metaphysics, or even ethics. There are also many other readings of 'Kant' with respect to this question of amphiboly, or the misuse of language. We need only mention the Semanticists, the Wittgensteinians, the Derridians, the Habermasians, the post-Marxists, etc. The 'linguistic turn' has brought language into the searchlight of philosophy, and writing generally, and increasingly, all expressive arts.

In the present context, amphiboly, as we have seen, refers to the mis-assignment of concepts to illegitimate *topoi*. The method by which such an amphibolous use of language is detected is *transcendental reflection*. Such a deliberation seeks to designate the domain in which the relations that are projected (identity and difference; agreement and disagreement; inner and outer; matter and form) can have legitimacy with respect to applicability or relevance. Beyond the logical questions of assignment, we can interpret this problematic of language as an echo of our earlier investigations of the source of the concepts, in light of the question of the status of imagination. And, indeed, we can see that this question is explicitly addressed in Kant's polemic against the rationalist Leibniz and the empiricist Locke. It is the confusion of the realms which incites the charge of amphiboly, and each of these philosophers is 'guilty'. Kant contends that Leibniz (and by extension, the Wolffians and Mendelssohn) confuses the realms by *intellectualising* sensibility, and that Locke (and by extension Hume) *sensualises* intelligibility in his empirical genealogy of concepts. It is the proper assignment of concepts to their own respective realms that allows us to undertake a self-examination of consciousness, its faculties, its *topoi* of significance, and its grounding in the transcendental unity of apperception.

The lessons of the *Inaugural Dissertation* have been repeated in the First *Critique*, and this repetition calls us to ask the question of the origins of expression, of conceptuality. Yet, if we emerge in the middle of a sentence, a conversation, and if questions of origins have been forbidden, how can we attain orientation in this world? How are we to deal with these perplexing questions and the ambiguous situations that assert themselves amid existence, in our own lives? How do we deal with our contrary, ambiguous world-views? In an attempt to honour these questions, we will turn to the transcendental dialectic of reason in order to trace the ground, the dimensions, of such a discordant harmony.

Study questions

1. In what sense is the phenomenon complex? How is Kant's notion different from the empirical object in Hume's philosophy?
2. Can there be knowledge of the noumena? If not, then how are we to apprehend or consider it?

TRANSCENDENTAL DIALECTIC (NKS 297; A293/B349)

Kant designates dialectic as a 'logic of illusion', the latter being a product of the judgment and not the senses. In this way, appearance as the representations of the sense is distinct from illusion, in that the former does not contain a judgment. Following upon his earlier designation of transcendental reflection as the assignment of representations and concepts to their own proper faculties of knowledge, Kant seeks to unmask a transcendental illusion which arises from the transgressive employment of principles beyond the limits of possible experience. In distinction to the transcendental employment of the principles of pure understanding which projects the schema for the application of concepts to sensibility, Kant identifies a *transcendent* deployment of principles beyond their proper *immanent* use and relevance.

We will see over the following pages that it is this transcendent transgression of principles beyond their immanent use which orchestrates the unavoidable dialectic of reason. The transgression specifically consists of regarding the connections evident in our own subjective consciousness as being at the same time objective connections in the things themselves. If we reflect upon our study of the First *Critique* thus far, especially in the disclosure of knowledge as the *a priori* synthetic field of objectification through time, space and the pure concepts of understanding, and of the necessary distinction of phenomenon and noumena, then we can readily ascertain that Kant is seeking to begin to apply the lessons of his 'Copernican Revolution' to various extant claims to knowledge.

It is clear for Kant that we cannot know things in themselves. And, further, it is claims of knowledge which pretend to knowledge of things themselves which are guilty of succumbing to the transcendental illusion. Echoing the first sentence of the A Edition, he regards this falling into illusion as an aspect of a natural dialectic of reason, which is not only inevitable, but is evident in the current sciences of his time (such as psychology, cosmology and theology, which he regards as pseudo-sciences). His own transcendental dialectic is meant as a critical attempt to not only expose illusions in our transcendental judgments, but also give us the means by which we can attempt to avoid illusion in the future, or at least be aware of it and come to terms with it in some way.

In light of this peculiarity of reason, Kant begins a discussion of its meaning as a *faculty of principles*, in distinction from understanding which he had defined earlier as a *faculty of rules* (mediate inferences). Knowledge from principles, he writes, is that 'knowledge alone in which I apprehend the particular in the universal through concepts. Thus every syllogism is a mode of deducing knowledge from a principle' (NKS 301). However, as these universal propositions (principles) are 'supported by pure intuition' and 'the conditions of the possibility of experience', knowledge through principles is not therefore based on the synthetic application of concepts (understanding), but upon 'thought alone' (NKS 303). This thought, Kant contends, has as its object the rules of the understanding, just as the object of the latter is appearance, to which its rules refer.

It is reason, never acting immediately upon objects, which gives unity to the manifold of experience by bringing unity to the understanding. What is crucial is that reason, although transcending the horizons of possible experience, is not therefore a mere illusion of the transcendent. The illusion arises, as we will recall, from the illegitimate application of pure understanding to the things themselves – which, though illegitimate, is still inevitable. The key distinction between understanding and reason therefore can be specified with the proviso that the former occurs in the modes of determination and reflection, while the latter takes place as inference. On this basis, Kant sets out concepts of reason, or the transcendental Ideas, as distinct from the pure concepts of the understanding. The difference, again, lies in the non-applicability of Ideas to phenomena, but only to the concepts and judgments of the understanding.

He compares these Ideas to those of Plato (from which he derives the expression) in that they transcend not only the sensible realm, but also that of the understanding and mathematical ideas. For instance, the Good is that which not only transcends the lower realms, but it is also in its light, as with reason itself, that the lower realms attain to the completeness of their intention. These Ideas are archetypes which state to that which is, what ought to be. In its freedom from the dimensions of sensibility and understanding, reason apprehends the totality of existence. Kant offers us a 'serial arrangement' of these various realms in the following schema, in which each level is subordinated to the higher representation:

Genus – Representation in general (representation)
Perception – Representation with Consciousness (*perceptio*)
Sensation – Representation as subjective modification of state (*sensatio*)
Knowledge – Objective perception (*cognitio*), either intuition or concept
  Intuition – relates to the singular
  Concept – refers to many with respect to a common aspect
    Empirical Concept – a concept arising from experience
    Pure Concept, or notion – concept arising from pure understanding
Concept of Reason, or *Transcendental Idea* – a concept formed of notions and transcending the possibility of experience. (NKS 314)

What Kant sets out here is a schema of the complicated demarcations of knowledge and its elements. It is similar to previous schemas and tables, but with the difference that reason is now explicitly included. The use of such a schema, as we will see in the sections on the Paralogisms and the Antinomies (not to mention the refutations of the proofs for the existence of a supreme Being), is to bring a precision and a discipline to our use of concepts and principles and to the appropriate locations for their deployment.

Although Kant admits that we have an almost natural propensity for error (as was the primary image of human existence in Nietzsche's philosophy), we may, by drawing precise lines and borders, be equipped to criticise transcendental judgments and dialectical inferences of pure reason. It is in this way that we may apprehend a more nuanced meaning of the criticism of pure reason as a mere play amongst concepts. It is not necessarily concerned about the play amongst concepts, but with a *mere* play that would suggest an uncritical and un-circumspective use of them. Yet, in the wake of such criticism, Kant feels that he can separate the wheat from the chaff as he is not seeking to curtail reason from its transcendental (or, as he will designate it, regulative) employment, especially as it pertains to the noumenal domain of freedom and practical morality. He is merely reminding us that all such endeavours are fraught with ambiguity and must be always accompanied by a critical evaluation of such employments.

The Transcendental Ideas are 'special *a priori* concepts' of reason which arise when the form of syllogism is 'applied to the synthetic unity of intuitions under the direction of the categories' (NKS 315). As we have already seen, this synthesis of intuitions is the product of the concept, the faculty of which is the understanding. The peculiar purpose of the Idea is to guide the understanding in its relation to 'experience in its totality' (NKS 315). The higher unity of reason (and the higher conflict) tends toward the universality of knowledge, and it attains this through inference, a judgment upon a judgment of the syllogism.

Kant writes that 'Caius is mortal' as a proposition could be determined via reflection upon experience of the understanding alone. However, a syllogism, and thus a judgment with *a priori* necessity and universality, requires a quite elaborate pathway to this conclusion. Indeed, we begin with the conclusion but seek the given judgment, a concept that is relatively more universal than Caius – or man – which is linked to the predicate of mortality, and state, 'All men are mortal', which becomes the major premise or the universal. It only requires someone to state, 'Caius is a man', to allow the judgment to be executed and the inference from the particular through the universal to the conclusion to be orchestrated without the direct action of reason upon experience. Indeed, reason only sees 'Man' or 'a man' but never Caius, as it is blind to singularity, or with Levinas, to the face.

Through this metaphor of the syllogism, Kant is seeking once again to distinguish reason from understanding. In this case, while understanding concerns the synthesis of intuitions, the transcendental concept of reason, or the Idea, invoking the universality of the major premise, is the 'allness (*universalitas*) or *totality* of the conditions for any given conditioned' (NKS 316).

Inference is a 'judging mediately', or a 'subsumption of the condition of a possible judgment under the condition of a given judgment' (NKS 320). The mediation is a step-by-step movement from more remote to nearer conditions. Kant gives the example of a conclusion, 'All bodies are alterable'. In this case, we move to the 'more remote' knowledge of the universal, 'All composites are alterable', which sets up the end-game of the conclusion. What these propositions share is the condition that is common to bodies and composites. If it is then stated, as the minor premise, that 'bodies are composites', we have a syllogism:

Major Premise	All composites are alterable
Minor Premise	Bodies are composites
Conclusion	Therefore, Bodies are alterable

The given judgment is the universal rule, or the major premise in the syllogism. The subsumption of a decided condition of a possible judgment (x is a composite) under the condition (all possible composites) of the universal gives rise to the minor premise. The *actual* judgment which projects the rule onto the subsumed case (as it could have been some other possible composite) is the *conclusion*.

Once again, through his metaphor of the syllogism, Kant contends that in its logical application, reason proceeds across a series of conditions, in this case, as the series of premises and the inferences that unite them. In its transcendental employment, as has been shown, reason speaks of conditions in a different sense. And, although Kant will defer discussions of the practical deployment of reason to 'the sequel', it is clear that there is yet another level to the acts of reason. Kant even suggests that reason in its various acts can serve to mediate theoretical reason with the domain of the practical through a series of conditions toward the perspective which apprehends the unconditional status of the series itself. But, even amidst this process of mediation, of reason seeking the conditioned or specificity and the conditioned seeking reason or completeness, reason stands outside as the unconditioned, wholly independent of the series and its conditions. But, even the series as a series, as a whole, is unconditioned, and is therefore for Kant, absolutely true.

In this way, Kant declares, the Idea is the unconditioned condition for the synthesis of the conditioned. The unconditioned itself, is the pure Idea of the Ideas, specified as three types of pure concepts of reason, the categorical synthesis in the subject, the hypothetical synthesis of a series and the disjunctive synthesis of aspects or parts of a system (the concepts of reason will be revisited shortly in our consideration of the 'Dialectical Inferences of Pure Reason').

These concepts are perhaps, Kant admits, without application to/in the concrete world, but are more properly designed to administer the understanding in its conceptual synthesis of the intuitive manifold. At the pinnacle of reason, Kant states with a long qualification, is the

Absolute, which is absolutely valid as it is not at all constricted by conditions. The transcendental Idea is 'directed' to the absolute totality, and 'leaves everything to the understanding' (NKS 318), which it surveys only with respect to the totality of the acts (of understanding) and seeks to trace a return, and thus, a grounding in the absolute as the unconditioned.

Through this tracing, there is exhibited an *isomorphic* unity of reason that underlies sensibility and understanding, and which blossoms as the unity of reason – of which understanding 'has no concept' (NKS 318). Reason brings the stems of sensibility and understanding, together with their root in imagination (Heidegger), into an absolute whole, an organic unity and system (although it would take the German Idealists to develop, in their varied ways, this idea of a system of pure reason).

Kant, so critical of all concepts which transgress the possibility of experience, now exalts to the absolute other concepts which also 'break the law tablets' (Nietzsche). He contends that the 'very little' that we say in the Idea, as a *maximum* indicates a problem to which there is no solution. Yet, its silence may be only in the domain of science. In fact, the distinctive demarcation of reason and understanding seems to have a more significant role, which was initially obscured with his forays into an extended metaphor for the universal in the logical form of the syllogism. Indeed, as already alluded to, a limit is set to theoretical understanding or understanding in order to make room for faith (and a different type of knowledge and expression).

Although it is the duty of reason to administer the understanding, yet, as *only an idea*, it can have no *immediate* application to a (theoretically defined) realm of experience. However, this peculiar restriction takes on another light in the domain of the practical, of the will and its direct determination by reason. Amid this *topos*, reason as the unconditioned in a realm without conditions, but only motives, maxims and acts, has an almost absolute hegemony. Its excession of power seeks to construct unities out of its own image in the will (Willkür) – by the action of the Wille (reason, in this sense), an act which is described as the self-determination of the Will. Kant contends:

Reason is here, indeed, exercising causality; and of such wisdom we cannot, therefore say disparagingly *it is only an idea*. On the contrary, just because it is the idea of the necessary unity of all possible ends, it must as an original, and at least restrictive condition, serve as standard in all that bears on the practical. (NKS 319)

I have already alluded to this other meaning of causality in my brief overview of the Second *Critique* and its intimation in the Third Antinomy. Yet, it is clear that the ideas of the former work already have an integral connection to the First *Critique* as a whole. This is the aforesaid *causality of freedom*, a free act/event distinct from the causality of a deterministic understanding. It is clear that with the differentiation of understanding from reason and the assignment to each of a specific *topos* for its legitimate and effective application, Kant lays the ground for a profound critical examination of the historicity of philosophical and scientific 'knowledge'. The primary criteria will be the jurisdiction and nativity of any concept to its appropriate domain, and this will be decided by an *act* of transcendental reflection, which is not merely a creature of syllogistic logic (a formal model of thought in one of its aspects), but is the event of 'thought alone'.

System of Transcendental Ideas – Laying the Ground for the Remainder of the Critique

When Kant spoke of being awoken from his dogmatic slumber by Hume, he was calling attention to the illicit extension of our concepts beyond the conditions of possible experience. However, as we have seen, he is intent on making a clear distinction between understanding and reason and their respective concepts. For, while there may be no extension of the former concepts, the latter do exhibit a capacity for expression that is beyond possible experience, even if this extension is problematic (and must therefore be subject to criticism). He speaks of concepts which have arisen from the nature of reason itself, and against which thinkers should be on their guard. But, as I have suggested, these concepts and their emergence are inevitable. The difficulty at the end of the day is one of logic: these concepts of reason have arisen on the basis of a necessary syllogism (NKS 327), and it is due to this apparent validity that we do not simply dismiss them out of hand. He describes a situation in which syllogisms without empirical premises are deployed to make conclusions about objects of which we have no concept. It is due to an unavoidable illusion that we ascribe objective validity to these objects, and this objective validity is, as we have seen, supported by the apparent validity of a necessary syllogism (although according to its procedure it is a pseudo-rational concept, as with Aristotle's definition in his *Poetics* of paralogism as a false inference from a consequent to an antecedent). Kant describes the variety of dialectical syllogisms, of which he states there are three, and which correspond to his previous outline of the three types of concepts of reason, or, Transcendental Ideas. This threefold differentiation is significant for the reader of the First *Critique* in that it gives her a prospective sketch of the main divisions of nearly the rest of the First *Critique*.

As we will recall, the three types of concepts are the categorical synthesis in the subject, the hypothetical synthesis of a series and the disjunctive synthesis of aspects or parts of a system. To each of these concepts corresponds a dialectical inference. The first inference, that of the transcendental *paralogism*, begins with the concept of the transcendental subject, which 'contains nothing manifold' (NKS 328), and thus is without any empirical premises. On this basis, it is concluded that the subject is an absolute unity, of which there is however no concept. The second inference, that of the *antinomy*, concerns the 'unconditioned synthetic unity of the series' (NKS 328). This type of inference leads to two mutually opposed interpretations of the same object. On the one hand, my concept (of the understanding) of the unity of the series leads to self-contradiction, while on the other, I fathom that there may be another way of conceiving of unity in the series, though without having a concept of such a unity. The third inference, that of the ideal of pure reason, postulates at the apex of the synthetic unity of all conditions, an *ensentium*, or a being of beings. This threefold differentiation of the dialectical inferences of pure reason lays the groundwork for the rest of Division One of the First *Critique*, the 'Transcendental Doctrine of the Elements'. It is divided between Kant's criticism of psychology in the Paralogisms, cosmology in the Antinomies, and theology in his refutations of the main proofs for the existence of God.

PARALOGISMS OF PURE REASON (NKS 328; A341/B399)

A paralogism, as suggested earlier, concerns a false inference from a conclusion to an antecedent. The tendency, moreover, of drawing such inferences, as we have seen, is endemic to the nature of reason. It cannot be avoided, Kant warns, but it may, he suggests, be 'rendered harmless'. The conclusion from which we begin in the context of the Paralogisms is the 'I think' as the formal condition of all thought. Yet, according to the nature of our reason, we begin to infer an object and character from this conclusion or consequent. Investigations of the inner experience of the 'I', or of apperception, Kant entitles a 'rational doctrine of the soul', a doctrine which seeks *a priori* knowledge of the soul beyond any reference to empirical reality. Kant lays out the *topos* for such a rational psychology according to the fourfold division of the table of categories (of the understanding):

1. The soul is substance.
2. The soul is simple.   3. The soul is a unity (identical).
4. The soul is in relation to possible objects in space.

From out of this fourfold division, the character of the soul is disclosed in the concepts of rational psychology: substance leads to *immateriality*; simplicity to *incorruptibility*; identity to *personality* – these three lead to a further notion of spirituality. The fourth, of possible relations in space, leads to notions of 'commercium with bodies' and to the notion that the soul is the 'principle of life in matter' (*anima*) and is the 'ground of animality'. Kant concludes this derivation of concepts with *immortality* which arises as a spiritual limitation of animality. From his perspective rational psychology is a pseudo-science in that it attributes objective reality to that which is impossible to know in the strict sense outlined above. For Kant, the 'I' merely indicates a transcendental subject which '$=X$'. It is unknown, just as is the transcendental object. Consciousness is not an object, but a form of representation, or a formal condition of thought. In this way, as seated in the transcendental subject, consciousness can only be apprehended as self-consciousness or of the consciousness of a self, apperception. There is no experience of a 'thinking being' – and if we seek, for Kant, to witness the 'play of our thoughts' as they do in fact occur, then we have immediately forsaken the transcendental standpoint and have entered empirical psychology, what he calls a 'physiology of the inner sense' (NKS 332). Yet, this would be to leave the ground of a rational psychology. He will therefore, without resorting to any empirical element, cast a critical eye upon the four paralogisms of pure rational psychology, those of substantiality, simplicity, personality and ideality. It should be stated, however, that the section on the Paralogisms was, as with the Transcendental Deduction, subject to differing accounts in the First and Second Editions of the First *Critique*. The fact of this restatement of the Paralogisms will be taken into account in the following examination.

Paralogisms: A Edition (NKS 333; A348)

First Paralogism: Of Substantiality

Kant criticises the notion that every subject is a trivial substance to the extent that, from the perspective of knowledge, it refers to no object. It merely states that 'I' am present to myself in all of my representations of consciousness. It is therefore redundant. Instead of empirical use, a rational concept of substance is merely an inference from the formal condition of thought, the 'I think' to a concept of a substance in which thought 'inheres'. The 'I' may be present in all of our thoughts, but it is not an intuition, an experience, and we cannot therefore infer the subsistence, below the 'I' of a substantial being. Or, we could and are driven to make such an inference, but it is fallacious to do so. We cannot have any pure knowledge of the subject, or indeed, infer from mere logical identity an existential substantiality.

Second Paralogism: Of Simplicity

Kant describes this paralogism as the contention that thought can never subsist in a composite or in many representations without a grounding in the 'absolute unity of a thinking subject' (NKS 336). And, while Kant himself will say much of the *a priori* unity of apperception, this latter, as an act, cannot be conceived as a simple substance. Not only is this once again beyond the horizons of possible experience, but it is faulty on its own 'logic'. If we depart from amid the multiplicity of representations, there is no way, Kant contests, to identify the simple substance as the unity of the thought; from our perspective amidst representations, there could well be other possible inferences or transcendental conditions of possibility, such as noumena, or other selves. Again, there is a false inference from a consequent or conclusion, the 'I think' of apperception, to an antecedent, in this case, a simple substance. Indeed, this paralogism is a misinterpretation of the *a priori* (non-empirical) character of apperception. Kant is willing to speak of simplicity in the sense of an *a priori* act outside of experience, but he is not willing to attribute it substantial being. We can only know the self *via negativa*.

Third Paralogism: Of Personality
As in his dealings with the previous two paralogisms, Kant contends that the paralogism of personality is yet again a false inference from the 'I think' as the formal condition of thought to an antecedent condition or concept of a numerically identical subject, or person. Indeed, in terms of my own knowledge, I refer all of my representations to a numerical substance as that which accompanies all representations, or in other words, which experiences time in its unity. Interestingly, Kant suggests that from the perspective of another subject, I myself will not appear permanent and may not even be considered to be identical as a being in time. In fact, as in the case of substantiality and simplicity, I will never have more than a negative conception of myself: I will only know myself as I appear, not as I may be in and of myself. The formal condition of thought serves as a referential framework for my knowledge and self-consciousness, but I cannot thereby infer either a numerically identical being or person or be assured of any permanence vis-à-vis flux of time. Nor can I truly extricate myself from this uncertainty, for my conscious awareness of my own numerical identity will not only not be corroborated by the other, but even by my own self in my own nonconscious states (sleep, etc.). This is a point which Schelling explored in his notion of the unconscious, especially in regard to the unconsciousness of spontaneous acts.

Fourth Paralogism: Of Ideality
Kant describes idealism as that type of thought which regards the existence of objects as problematic. In other words, our immediate perception is that of which we are certain, and our notion of an object corresponding or causing this perception is merely an inference to which is attached an uncertainty. However, Kant uses this aura of uncertainty in order to underline his own conception of transcendental idealism as distinct from empirical idealism, and with significant consequences. The former type of idealism is that to which our attention has be focused for some time. It is the notion that the empirical reality is real, but is interpreted as a mode of representation of consciousness, which itself is an aspect of self-consciousness. This mode

of consciousness is appearance and is known immediately to us. Beyond this appearance is no-thing, a vague conception of a transcendental object = X. It is not susceptible to knowledge. Kant distinguishes his philosophy from that of those he calls transcendental realists, who simply posit the realm of externality, or empirical objects, as existing in and for themselves. For him, this is a transgression of the horizons of possible experience and gives rise to a quite ironic situation for the realist. For he contends, that, in addition to the positing of objects in and for themselves, the realist also distinguishes these objects from the sensations which apprehend them.

However, with this distinction, there arises an epistemological fallacy which attempts to coordinate the objects with the senses of objects. This fallacy gives rise to a form of empirical idealism as the methodological practice of the realist, as for instance in both Hume and Locke. Kant contends that the additional and unwarranted inference of the reality of the object from the sensation of the object leads us away from a criticism of pure reason to a side show which is merely another instance of paralogism. He has no such problems as he regards the empirical domain as mere appearance, but as it is all there is, as at once transcendentally ideal (through the projections of time, space and concept) and empirically real, as representations of my consciousness. This solution is possible in that, for Kant, these kinds and modes of representations exist only 'for us'. But, even as we cannot know the thing-in-itself, this is not the loss of a notion of an external object beyond the delusion of our senses, but of a noumena which has no relevance to theoretical reason. Empirical objects, as representations in space, time and order, are real, even though their possibility is ideally constituted by the *a priori* conditions of consciousness.

Kant contends that rational or transcendental psychology as a science is abortive, that its claims to have extended our knowledge (or to have given us certainty) are false. Indeed, there is nothing that is not in flux excepting the mere indication of 'I', which has nothing in itself which is manifold. It is a merely formal condition of thought, an effect from which no inference can be made as to its substantial existence. The 'I' as a form of consciousness is an act and it is through a phenomenology of these acts of inner experience that the temporal and spatial character of the self is disclosed. Rational psychology, however, shrinks back from this vision of flux and seeks, by transgressing the horizons of possible experience, everlasting eternities. It transgresses its own appropriate domain, that of temporal existence, and seeks an unconditioned unity at the heart of every condition, and in this case, of the 'I'. However, it is only reason which is unconditioned, but in being unconditioned, it thereby exiles itself from the immanent domain of theoretical reason or understanding. Kant, having forsaken a positive answer to the riddle of the world, seeks only to set reason free from 'sophistical theories'. The implications of his transcendental idealism are quite profound, especially with respect to the vast kingdom of traditional metaphysics, and indeed, with respect to the possibility of ever knowing, in the strict sense, in this life or beyond, anything at all with regard to the thing-in-itself. What is interesting is that his criticisms of rational psychology become an essential part of his own philosophy, not as demonstrations of an argument or of the refutation of other philosophies, but as species of fallacious argument and judgment that arise from reason by necessity. Thus, the exposition of the paralogism is in truth the self-disclosure of reason in its manifest event.

Paralogisms: B Edition (NKS 368; B406)

Kant, at the outset of his restatement of the syllogisms, announces that he must consider with a 'critical eye', and in one continuous exposition, the 'predicaments' of a pure psychology which seeks to transgress the horizons of possible experience. In this way, we can detect perhaps a superficial difference with A in its jettisoning of the four paralogisms, considered separately. He does, however, proceed to set out four numbered sub-divisions in his first section. In the first division, he states that 'I' am the 'determining subject of that relation which constitutes the judgment' (NKS 368). And we may even venture to call this determining subject the subject proper. He contends that on the basis of this 'apodeictic and identical proposition', we cannot infer the existence of a 'subsistent being' or 'substance'. This can be readily seen as a repetition of the first paralogism in the A edition. Similarly, in the second division, Kant repeats, in a very brief fashion, the prohibition on moving from the analytic judgment that the 'I' as apperception is simple to the fallacious antecedent of a *simple substance*. He contests that such a proposition would be synthetic as substance is always associated with intuitions, and 'in me' these are sensible. The pattern of brief repetition of the A edition continues, and just as briefly, with the denial of the concept of personality, as an identical substance, as an inference made upon the basis of the analytic identity of the subject in time. Once again, in division four, Kant denies any possible knowledge of the self in distinction from its interaction with objects, or from its nexus of representations. There is no experience of the self, and thus, we cannot contend that the self is a 'thinking being' that could subsist outside of the labyrinth of things. In each of these denials of substance, it would seem that Kant merely reaffirms that which was outlined in the A edition.

Kant, prefiguring what is perhaps the real reason for his radical abbreviation of the paralogism, suggests that his entire project would be in danger if there were someone who could prove, *a priori*, that thinking beings are simple substances. It could be contended, he muses, that such a notion would be the fruit of an *a priori* synthetic judgment, but one not applied to the senses through understanding and schematism, but upon the things in themselves, amid the noumena. He describes rational or pure psychology as resting on the fallacious syllogism that concludes that the thinking being is a substance, not from any reference to the conditions of possible experience, but from mere identification of the subsumed case with the subject as substance. Once again, Kant drives home his contention that the concept of a subject cannot be coordinated with an intuition, and thus, with objective reality. And, along with substance, each of the other concepts of pure or rational psychology also falls.

The real reason for Kant's abbreviation of his criticisms of pure psychology is exhibited in the next section which is entitled, 'Refutation of Mendelssohn's Proof of the Permanence of the Soul'. Indeed, this discussion takes up almost the rest of the B Paralogism, excepting a brief conclusion and a transition to the Antinomies, i.e., from psychology to cosmology. Kant begins with a criticism of Plato in his supposition of a simple and immortal soul. He admits that this soul is simple and therefore changeless if we only take into account its non-composite character. Yet, Kant points out, echoing Leibniz, that the soul may still have an intensive quantity and thus a degree of reality to its existence, and this would imply that the differences in the soul would allow the possibility of an alteration in its existence. It would therefore no longer be changeless, immortal, nor simple. He contends that the immortal soul may be turned into nothing by a languishing, by a 'gradual loss of its powers' (NKS 373). And, in fact, from the perspective of inner sense, such a soul is 'undemonstrated' and 'indemonstrable' (NKS 373).

Kant, without mentioning Mendelssohn once in this section, proceeds to further amplify his conclusions with respect to the paralogisms with the contention that there is no way or means of acquiring knowledge of the subject 'so far as the possibility of its existence is concerned' (NKS 376). In this way, the thinking subject is inaccessible to knowledge in that it is determining and not determined, a spontaneous act of the 'indeterminate proposition, "I think" ' (NKS 377). But, again, such a misunderstanding is understandable and arises, for Kant, from the natural dialectic of reason with itself. It is the attempt to close the circle, to make the subject into an object, even though objectivity itself depends upon the subject as the unconditioned act at the heart of the unity of self-consciousness (a unity of thought and not of intuition). If the subject became object, if it were deemed to be a substance, there would no longer be objects, which is an impossibility.

Kant intensifies his criticism of rational psychology by calling it a deception, a falsity that will 'destroy itself in the attempt at fulfilment' (NKS 378). And, once again, the primary import of Kant's criticisms, as with the longer A Edition, is negative, in this case, as a clearing of the ground of a hydra of misinterpretations and received dogmas and doctrines, each grounded in the notion of substance and maintained through a discipline which forbids investigations of the being of the soul in the world, even if still *a priori* in Kant's sense. What is at stake for Mendelssohn is, after all, Kant suggests, the question of the immortality of the soul, and of Plato's solution to the question. It is no wonder that Mendelssohn thought Kant had 'destroyed everything', when through the latter's critical and transcendental method all that he most cherished simply vanished.

The difficulty of rational psychology is that it attempts to make a being out of reason, that from the 'I' which is attained through abstraction, there is posited a rational being or substance with an existence outside of sensibility, matter and time. For Kant, there is no such object, and none will be found. However, in his transition from psychology to cosmology, to the Antinomies, Kant expresses the possibility of a positive deployment of reason beyond the conditions of possible experience as that of the legislative practical reason which has its own rational principle distinct from theoretical reason and the sensible deployments of the understanding. But, this is not the positing of a substantial being, as it is only theoretical reason that seeks to determine an object.

Rational psychology fails because it has not limited reason in order to make room for faith. It is significant that Kant makes this suggestion before his treatment of the Antinomies, for it is here that we will begin to fathom the possibility of reason as a hidden unity directing itself to various regions or topologies of its concern, as in this present case, between theoretical and practical reason. This is especially the case in the Third Antinomy, which, as I will argue, allows for the thesis of a causality of freedom, one distinct from that of the understanding. Moreover, as we have seen, there is also aesthetic and teleological reason, another topology of reason, but one that sought to disclose a unity amidst the regions as a whole under the administration of a diversified and mature reason.

THE ANTINOMY OF PURE REASON (NKS 384; A405/B432)

As we will recall, the second of the dialectical inferences of pure reason, that of *antinomy*, concerns the 'unconditioned synthetic unity of the series'. Kant regarded the paralogism as a one-sided illusion, as there was never the real chance of a counter-assertion in the domain of the subject (i.e. the subject does not exist). Antinomy, on the contrary, refers to a 'natural antithetic' of assertions and counter-assertions. In its search for an unconditioned unity, reason, when applied to the field of objective appearances, gives rise to differing rational accounts of the unconditioned unity. Kant claims that this is a 'new phenomenon of human reason' (NKS 385). We should here step back and consider Kant's opening statements in the Preface to the First *Critique* in which he speaks of the war of attrition that was metaphysics.

We will see, as we have already indicated with respect to the purpose of the Transcendental Dialectic, that Kant is seeking to absorb this very war of attrition into his transcendental philosophy, to be disciplined and regulated by his architectonic of reason. The war itself is a phenomenon of reason and therefore must become a thread in the grand tapestry of reason. Whatever we do comes to define us as a phenomenon.

Concepts arise only from understanding, yet a concept can be, Kant suggests, set free for deployment beyond possible experience. He suggests that reason may demand that unconditioned unity, or absolute totality, be a condition for the existent object, the conditioned. This demand allows for a pathway from the operations of the understanding amid the series of conditions and conditioned to the unconditioned. In this way, the concept becomes a Transcendental Idea, and the unity that is achieved for the series of conditions is only possible amid the *topos* of the Idea. The demand is further specified as one which demands that for every conditioned, there be the entirety of conditions and the absolutely unconditioned. Kant suggests that this is merely an extension of concepts to the unconditioned and that only categories which are associated with the subordination of series of conditions to one another (as with the moments of time, unlike the coordination of space) will be 'fitted' to an extension to the unconditioned.[27]

Kant names the synthesis of the series which passes from the nearest condition to the farthest the *regressive synthesis*, and it is this synthesis which seeks the initial conditions for the conditioned, the first of course being the unconditioned. Kant lays out the system of cosmological ideas through a derivation from the four categorical divisions, quantity, quality (Mathematical), relation and modality (Dynamic).

In the first instance, he extends the meaning of the antinomy, as seeking antecedent conditions, to that of being concerned with *past time*. Space itself also discloses itself as a succession of appearances and thus exhibits, through the prism of time, mutual limitations arising between each and every part of space. In this way, time and space, as the quanta of our intuition, will form the *topos* of the first of the cosmological ideas, that of *Composition*. Matter is susceptible to a regressive synthesis as its parts are its remote conditions, and thus serves as the *topos* of the second idea, that of *Division*. Of the categories which fit into the cosmological synthesis of the series from the conditioned to the unconditioned, it is only the category of causality which meets both of the conditions, that of susceptibility to forming a series and that of subordination. Causality leads to the third idea, that of *Origination*. The last idea, *Dependence of Existence*, arises from the modality which ceaselessly reveals the dependence, amid temporality, of every conditioned on another conditioned. Yet, that which reason demands is the absolute completeness or totality of each of these cosmological ideas, indeed, such totality is built into the idea as Idea.

What is sought is not only a unity of the series of conditions in accord with the concepts for the understanding, but also an unconditioned totality, or completeness, which Kant significantly contends is the work of the imagination, but remains only an idea. Such a role for imagination calls to mind our earlier excursions into the A and B Deductions and the demotion of imagination in the latter. It would seem that such a role would make the imagination, at least in this transcendental sense, incompatible with the domain of empirical synthesis under the rules of the understanding. Moreover, if indeed Heidegger is correct to suggest that reason *is* transcendental imagination (as Hamann had also suggested), there arise unavoidable questions as to the role of the transcendental imagination in the Second *Critique* (despite the elimination of the empirical or reproductive imagination). Yet, this question transcends the horizons of the present Reader's Guide.

The unconditioned is the apex of the regressive synthesis through which we seek to give completeness to the successive synthesis of the manifold of intuition. But, what is the unconditioned? Kant lays out two senses or meanings for the unconditioned. On the one hand, it is a series in which only the totality of the series is unconditioned. On the other hand, it is a member of a series, and every other member is subordinated to it. The first series is without limit, without beginning and whole – it is infinite, and thus, the regression can never be complete. The second series designates one being amongst other beings as the *arché*, and it is attributed as beginning, limit, simple, self-active (free), and as natural necessity.

The *ground*, whether world (mathematics), nature (dynamics) or *something else besides* is the condition for the existence of empirical objects, for appearances. And, as the ground, or condition, Kant suggests, it is also the cause, which is either unconditioned causality, or freedom, or conditioned causality in the sense of a natural cause. The former is necessary while the latter is contingent. Even natural necessity is merely the 'unconditioned necessity of appearances' (NKS 393).

However, in this scenario, in terms of the two senses of the unconditioned, we will have two interpretations of the ground of knowledge, and there will thus arise the antithetic of pure reason. An antithetic is a war of attrition between doctrines, in which no superiority or lasting hegemony can be obtained. From the standpoint of the Critical Philosophy this situation of conflict itself becomes a phenomenon for the self-exposition and critique of pure reason. The conflict itself involves combatants which have similar claims to legitimacy, and similar bases of power, and thus from a logical perspective there would seem to be no cure for such a malady. Kant assents that there is no cure, but, since we know this, we must learn to detect and deal with the *necessary illusions* which arise from the nature of dialectical reason. The problem is expressed in one way by the fact that understanding can never realise the Ideas of reason, while reason must never concern itself with particularity.

Kant already tells us that there is no solution to this conflict, but he advocates that the conflict be regulated within the rule-structure of the architectonic of reason. Yet, rules are ceaselessly, inexorably broken. In the four Antinomies, Kant will lay out four basic types of rule-breaking, or transgression. Yet since thought, even dogmatic thought, is a natural dialectic of reason, it seems problematic to suggest that our very acts of reason are somehow 'guilty'. Indeed, Kant does not seek to punish the transgressors, nor does he seek to assert the truth of one combatant over another, in some sort of unconditional or even conditional surrender. Instead, he seeks, *in the first instance*, to provoke the conflict, to set it up for all to see (the *sceptical method* distinct from *scepticism*). In an almost Derridean format, Kant lays out assertion and counter-assertion, together with each of their extended arguments, side by side on the same page. In the wake of the exposure of the fallacies and limitations of each of the positions (if taken as a Spinozist, monistic absolute), Kant seeks to show how each assertion and counter-assertion pertains to its own domain of relevance, of jurisdiction, or that each is a sovereign region within the system of human knowledge.

It is the assignment via transcendental reflection of concepts to their appropriate domains, in such a manner, which preserves the integrity of the logical (lawful) paradigm in which each is operating, but introduces a differentiation of the *topos* of each of their respective concerns. We will now turn to the Antinomies proper in order to examine Kant's transcendental method in practice. I will examine each of these positions in turn, their respective proofs, and Kant's observation and makeshift resolution of the conflict, a flashpoint amid this war of attrition.

The First Antinomy (NKS 396; A426/B454)
Thesis:

The World has a beginning in time, and is also limited in space.

Antithesis:

The World has no beginning, no limits in space, and is infinite.

This first conflict of reason, or the quantitative, mathematical antinomy, concerns the beginning and limits of the world. It *either* has a beginning and is spatially limited, *or*, it has no beginning or spatial limits, it is infinite and unlimited with respect to time and space. Most of us believe or think we know that there was a beginning of the world, either vis-à-vis the mythical scenarios of the major religions, or as the Big Bang of science (what kind of designation is this for the event of either creation or Being?). There were also those others, as with the early Greeks, who do not posit a beginning, but instead affirm a variant of an eternal recurrence of the same, as Nietzsche echoes millennia later. In each case, the enemy combatant can and must establish his rights. Regarding the former claimant, if there was no beginning, there would be only eternal recurrence, but, one that would never be able to complete even one of its instances, and thus, it could never recur, since such an event would presuppose a completion of the former state. Therefore, there must be a beginning of nature and world. With respect to the latter claimant, any beginning must be preceded by an antecedent time, but this time would be empty, and could never give rise to a world. Therefore, the world can have no beginning. As Kant observes, each of the assertions can muster arguments in its defence, and our inability to decide between them constitutes a serious problem. Kant will set forth a solution to the cosmological dialectic in 'The Interest of Reason in these Conflicts' and following sections, which we will consider below.

The Second Antinomy (NKS 402; A434/B462)
Thesis:

Every composite substance in the world is made up of simple parts, and nothing anywhere exists save the simple or what is composed of the simple.

Antithesis:

No composite thing in the world is made up of simple parts, and there nowhere exists in the world anything simple.

The second conflict of reason, or the qualitative, mathematical antinomy, concerns the quality of the world with respect to the question of the possible existence of simple parts from which composites arise. As with the first Antinomy, each assertion is able to stake its claim to legitimacy over against the other. But, instead of regarding this as yet another embarrassment of reason, Kant undertakes to examine yet another region of conflict in the dialectical self-exposition and critique of reason. The Thesis argues that if there were no simple parts, there could then be no composites, and thus, the denial of simple parts leads to Nothing. This proof concludes that simples must exist, and that composites are external relations of these simples, which while distinct as substances, may not exist outside of the manifold of composition. The Antithesis, on the contrary, argues that if we assume that composites are made up of simples, we immediately run into difficulties. For each part of a composite, as a being in space, must itself occupy space. However, if the simple was to occupy space, it would be subject to the routine divisions to which space is always susceptible. In this way, there would be no simples in the world. Again, we have a seemingly irresolvable conflict, which indicates that there must be a solution to the dialectic of reason. Of course, we cannot still the dialectic, but in order to preserve the unity of reason, we must seek a way to read these conflicts as capable of regulation. We will consider Kant's solution in the guise of his transcendental idealism below.

The Third Antinomy (NKS 409; A444/B472)
Thesis:

Causality in accordance with the laws of nature is not the only causality from which the appearances of the world can one and all be derived. To explain these appearances it is necessary to assume that there is also another causality, that of freedom. (A444, B472)

Antithesis:

There is no freedom; everything in the world takes place solely in accordance with laws of nature. (A445, B473)

We have already been given a distinct indication that there is more to existence, to the world, than theoretical reason and its nexus of representational consciousness. This difference amidst existence was announced earlier as phenomenon and noumena. It is in the third conflict of reason, or the dynamical antinomy of relation, however, that our most explicit exit/access point is disclosed in the futile battle between freedom and determinism. The domain to which we will have access will be that of the practical aspect of a unified reason. In this section, therefore, we will follow the pathway by which we gain entry into this domain.

An antinomy, as I have indicated above, is a conflict which arises from the inner nature of Reason itself. Such conflict erupts between two transcendental Ideas, each of which have arisen from reason with equal legitimacy. However, as each has its own stated legitimacy, the conflict becomes symptomatic of a self-contradiction of reason, which occurs as a thought event which has the character of a limit situation. The limit asserts itself as each of the ideas, though legitimate, are mutually exclusive. In other words, their very juxtaposition threatens to violate each of the laws of logic, that of identity, contradiction and excluded middle. It is the fourth law of logic which will give us a clue to the solution of the state of antinomy.

In the Introduction to the First *Critique*, Kant laments the battlefield of metaphysics in which such ideas wage war without ever gaining a single inch of territory in either direction. Indeed, no territory can be gained in that these ideas are in a state of total contradiction. Only the total annihilation of one by the other would end the war, or so it would seem. (Hegel for his part, in his well-known triadic schema, sought a higher synthesis under the motto, 'Think Contradiction!') For, on the one hand, the Thesis states that there exist differing types of causality which are effective in the world, while, on the other hand, the Antithesis states that there is no freedom in the world. For Kant, since these ideas arise from the very inner nature of reason itself, any total victory of one over the other would necessarily be impossible. However, the persistence of this situation of conflict is a painful embarrassment for a faculty which is alleged to be characterised by unity. How could such a self-contradictory faculty which exudes conflictual ideas from its own nature have the regal air of authority? At the same time, it is not necessary, in Kant's eyes, to have to chose between the two extremes. But, that in no way means that the solution is to enact a synthesis between the two. Instead, Kant attempts to resolve the antinomy through a consideration of the concept of 'world' which is indicated in both the Thesis and the Antithesis. In the Thesis, it could be argued that Kant is suggesting a 'world' that includes within itself differing types of causality. This calls to mind Schopenhauer's designation of the world as will and representation, as freedom and causality. The Antithesis, on the contrary, depicts a world in which one type of causality operates, that of the principle of sufficient reason. The Thesis may not seem to necessarily exclude the latter causality, but does so with its insistence that a causality of freedom be also extant in the world. Moreover, the causality of determinism could never assent to such a co-habitation. As neither of the two ideas can gain total supremacy, but as the conflict burns on nevertheless, Kant is forced to find some resolution which will preserve the integrity of each of the ideas, and thus, to preserve the unity which is at the foundation of the authority of reason. As they cannot co-exist, and as they cannot be synthesised without being nullified in their essential determinations, there must be a disclosure of the world in which the two can both exist, but in differing domains. The causality of determinism articulates the iron series of the nexus of representations; it is the organising principle of the empirical dimension of the phenomenon. The causality of freedom exists in that sphere of the world which transcends the nexus of representations, in a *topos* outside of time, space and causality, outside of the principle of sufficient reason. While the necessity of a 'solution' to the antinomy occurs on the basis of routine logical argumentation, the actual solution transcends the sphere of representation through a projection of a transcendental realm, the noumenon, simultaneous but distinct from the web of appearances. The projection of differing domains allows for a compartmentalisation of each of the ideas to its own sphere of applicability or meaning. Moreover, it allows for a more complex understanding of the world as that which can abide differing dimensions amidst its own unified totality. In this way, the world is neither an anarchic flux of random appearances, nor is it a tight chain of causally ordered 'things'. Instead, the world is articulated as the transcendental architectonic of reason in its various spheres of relevance, those of the phenomenon and the noumenon being the most obvious. Moreover, as we have seen, it is not as if there is no relation of the one to the other, or vice versa. As Kant has explicitly stated, the noumenon is the transcendental condition of possibility for the phenomenon, but this relationship should be seen as one of neither physical nor metaphysical causation (conceived as a causality of determinism), nor one which asserts an epistemological encounter. There is nothing we can *know* of the noumenon since knowledge pertains only to the domain of the phenomenon; we cannot even 'really' imagine it. We think (non-knowing, as Bataille would have put it) the thing-in-itself, and we think and act practically in the domain of this intimacy. This is thus the explanation for the contention that in the Kantian philosophy we are double-headed. We exist amidst the world, but we each must see the world always, and simultaneously, with differing eyes, those of theory, practice, aesthetics, teleology. It is a specific regionality of Reason which, for Kant, ultimately unifies our *multiplications*, as it exists as the root for these stems, through its persistent indiscretion with the imagination.

To understand more fully what Kant has unfolded so far, we would need to consider this antinomy of freedom in relation to the Second *Critique*, which has been briefly outlined above. In this light, we would be able to fill out the content to our meta-distinction between the phenomenon and noumenon, and begin to scrutinise the limits of theoretical reason from a place to which it has no applicability or relevance, although this place stills abides, for Kant, in the house of reason. However, while the reader is encouraged to take up the *Critique of Practical Reason* (1786) in this context, we will now continue our reading of the First *Critique* with an examination of the Fourth Antinomy.

The Fourth Antinomy (NKS 415; A452/B480)

Thesis:

There belongs to the world, either as its part or as its cause, a being that is absolutely necessary.

Antithesis:

An absolutely necessary being nowhere exists in the world, nor does it exist outside the world as its cause.

The fourth conflict of reason, or the dynamical antinomy of modality, concerns the existence of an absolutely necessary being in the world. We will recall that this question was raised above with respect to the relation between the series and the unconditioned. Is the series itself in its totality unconditioned, or is a member of the series itself an unconditioned vis-à-vis subordination and hegemony? The two possibilities of the meaning of the unconditioned once again play themselves out in the dialectic of reason. The Thesis argues that as the world contains, as sensible, a series of alterations, then for any conditioned, we will be able to trace the series of conditions for these changes until we reach the unconditioned, which is the only condition which is absolutely necessary. In light of this dependence of alteration upon the absolute condition, an absolutely necessary 'something' must exist. And, this something must exist in the sensible world, in time, or we would not be able to trace the series of conditions to completion. The Antithesis argues that a necessary being exists neither inside nor outside the world by highlighting the problems which arise if we assume such a necessary being. If there is a necessary being, there is either a beginning to the series which is without a cause, or the series is without beginning and while none of its parts are necessary, it is itself necessary in and of itself. The Antithesis contends that the first possibility is in conflict with the restriction of causation to horizons of time, while the second possibility is self-contradictory since a whole cannot be necessary if it is composed of merely unnecessary parts. Neither could a necessary being exist outside of the world for at the instant of its act of beginning it has itself entered time. In this way, there can be no necessary being inside or outside the world, nor can the world itself be deemed necessary if it is regarded as merely composed of the unnecessary. Again, we have a conflict which is irresolvable on its own terms. This particular conflict moreover, as we will see below, will play itself out in our investigation of the third and final dialectical inference of pure reason, that of the *Ideal of Pure Reason*. Yet, before turning to Kant's refutation of all variants of theology, we will examine his own solution to the dialectical conflict of reason. It will be in the context of a solution to the problems inherent in reason that Kant will more fully articulate his conception of transcendental idealism. And, in his consideration of theology, we will see the radical implications of this new array of philosophical weapons in the age of criticism.

The Interest of Reason in these Conflicts (NKS 422; A462/B490)

The four conflicts of reason describe the 'four series of synthetic presuppositions which impose *a priori* limitations on the empirical synthesis' (NKS 422). In each case, the ongoing syntheses of conditions in each domain is led by reason to the unconditioned in its attempt to see all as a totality. The difficulty arises that that which it is attempting to witness can only be apprehended as conditioned, from within the horizons of possible experience. In this way, there can be no answers to the questions associated with the conflict of reason, questions of origin, simplicity, freedom, and the existence of a supreme being – though we are ceaselessly haunted by these questions. Since we are in a seeming double-bind, Kant considers whether the 'origin or this conflict, whereby it is divided against itself, may not have arisen from a mere misunderstanding' (NKS 423). We should not, and cannot however, chose one combatant over another, but must attempt to understand their positions and their interests. On this basis, we will learn what the interests of reason are in these disputes.

Kant characterises each of the sides as consistent representations of two diverse positions, the Thesis being that of *dogmatism* (rationalism) and the Antithesis that of *empiricism*. The former seems to fulfil our practical interests (immortality, etc.), speculative interests (an *a priori* knowledge), and, Kant suggests, it thereby has also popularity in its favour. The latter on the contrary seems to undermine the practical and speculative interests of rationalism. It would thus be quite unpopular to 'every well-disposed man' (NKS 424). Yet, while empiricism does undermine the practical and the *a priori* of the speculative, it yields access to the empirical manifold which allows the understanding to operate within the horizons of possible experience as science. Kant acknowledges the service empiricism performs in stripping the pretensions of Ideas to have relevance to the domain of possible experience, or of its seduction of understanding to transgress its own limits. Yet, he criticises what he calls a dogmatic empiricism which would deny Ideas altogether, even those which were operating in their own appropriate domain. Once again, we cannot choose one side or the other, but must see their dispute as a 'misunderstanding', a conflict that can be resolved through the assignment by reason of each faculty of knowledge to its most appropriate place within the architectonic, or possible system, of reason.

However, the establishment of such an administration or regime of reason seems quite impossible due to the denial by empiricism of all grounds of authority, a denial which makes any system impossible. It is in this way, Kant suggests, that we may prefer, for the sake of the interests of reason, to side with the Thesis. If there were no practical interests involved there may be no reason to choose one or the other. Yet, this is not the case. However, Kant attempts a solution that does not merely choose sides, but seeks to allow each of the opposing assertions to find their own respective place in his transcendental idealism. It is to this solution that we will now turn.

Solutions of the Conflicts of Reason with Itself (NKS 430; A476/B504)

Kant states that transcendental philosophy, uniquely among the sciences, should be able to answer the cosmological questions that it itself has raised, and the questions should be able to be answered exclusively within the domain of the Idea. This is even more the case since the Idea is not only prohibited from the empirical domain, but is also forbidden to become manifest as an object, or substance, through the intervention of the understanding. The answers refer only to the 'absolutely unconditioned totality of the synthesis of appearances' (NKS 434), which can never be found within the realm of possible experience. But, if the object fails to arise which discloses the idea, Kant suggests that the failure lies with the idea itself. He asks, 'Whence come those ideas, the solution of which involves us in such difficulty?' (NKS 434). What demands a completed synthesis and an absolute totality? As such a drive will not find its satisfaction in experience, and as the drive cannot be quieted, we are guided to a critical solution of the conflicts which considers the questions 'in relation to the foundation of the knowledge upon which the question is based' (NKS 435).

The basis of the distinction between foundations rests, for Kant (and here we can see the influence of Hume) on the criterion of a possible empirical concept. In other words, if the concept does not find its reality in possible experience, then it is an idea, a thought-entity. It is in the making of this distinction that we may begin to liberate reason and its rightful employment from the dogmatic fictions, whether rational or empirical.

As we have already hinted, and have been laying the ground for, transcendental idealism proposes a solution to the conflicts of reason. This doctrine posits two dimensions of existence, the phenomenon and the noumena. All questions which confuse realists and dogmatists alike are confined and answered in the former dimension, that of sensibility, imagination and understanding. Any attempt to transgress beyond the phenomenon, and to speak of things themselves, renders knowledge impossible. Indeed, all that we can attribute to the transcendental object is spontaneity, as a pure intelligible cause of appearances, but Kant suggests that this is done 'merely in order to have something corresponding to sensibility viewed as a receptivity' (NKS 441). However, the lure to transgression remains, even in the very notion of the conditioned, as the disclosure of its totality of conditions is '*set* us *as a task*' (NKS 443). Such a task is legitimate if it remains within the circle of the phenomenon, it is only its escape from the circle that initiates conflicts. Indeed, any actual attempt to trace the totality of conditions would, for the phenomenal finite being, eventually *break down*, thereby revealing the mask of the universal, or the major premise of the syllogism, which gives timeless and bodiless answers, conditions, to that which is necessarily temporal and embodied.

In this way, the task set by reason must be regarded as a *problem* of reason and not in the manner of an axiom. In other words, the task must be regarded as merely regulative, guiding us in what we ought to do, but having in and of itself no *a priori* knowledge of the object sought, such as was the case with the pseudo-rational assertions of substance, etc. Moreover, even though it sets this task, such a task can never be fulfilled as its fulfilment would be a transgression beyond the possibility of experience, into nothing – a place where even substance cannot abide.

Reason and understanding, as with Leibniz, move in differing orbits, as Kant has relentlessly argued for over two hundred pages. And it is this recognition which will allow us to disclose a solution to the conflict of reason with itself. The meaning of reason has changed into a regulative reason which is grounded upon its exile from the sensible domain. Kant proposes a solution to each of the questions of reason, a solution that is based upon his prior development of the distinction between the phenomenon and noumena. His solutions seem to arise from a delicate negotiation between the sides, one that clarifies the jurisdiction of each claim to knowledge through a critical examination of these claims. We should recall, in terms of our method of analysis, the distinction between the mathematical and the dynamical inferences of reason. For as we will ascertain, each of these types of Ideas and of their respective conflicts admits of differing types of solutions.

To the question of a beginning, Kant, seemingly giving in to the Antithesis, gives the answer that the world has no beginning, nor limit in space. This accords with the criteria of possible experience. However, he denies the other assertion of the Antithesis that the world is infinite, in that he regards this as transcending the horizons of possible experience, and proposes instead an indefinite process of appearance. The world itself, Kant contends, cannot ever be known as complete, and cannot therefore be attributed limits, either conditionally or unconditionally.

With respect to the question of simplicity, Kant seems to come down once again with the Antithesis, that there are no absolutely simple parts. He sets out the paradox that suggests that even though there may be an aggregate, a 'whole', there before us, the requirement of reason for an infinite division *on the way to the simple* can, within the horizon of possible experience, never give rise to an infinity of simple parts. Indeed, the parts only exist and arise during the division. As with the case of space, an object may be *infinitely divisible* without having *infinitely many parts*. Yet, as the criteria is that of possible experience, Kant cautions the adherents of the Antithesis with the possibility of experiencing such ultimate parts, arguing that any such disclosure would have to take place amidst possible experience, and be regarded by the regulative reason as never absolutely completed, indeed, incapable of completion.

Kant points out the there is a difference in the manner of solution of the conflicts of reason with respect to their type, whether mathematical or dynamical. The former confine themselves to the domain of appearance only, and in both cases, Kant denies both sides of the dispute, and negotiates an answer to the satisfaction of neither party. The conflicts of reason of a dynamical nature, however, Kant suggests, can be resolved to the satisfaction of both parties in that instead of a homogeneous domain, there can be admitted *heterogeneous* domains in regards to causality (Relation) and the relation of the necessary and the contingent (Modality). In other words, while the homogeneous condition for the mathematical antinomies was that of sensibility, the dynamical antinomies are oriented to the heterogeneity of conditions, of the sensible as the series of conditions, and that which is purely intelligible, and thus, *alterior* to the series. We should immediately call to mind the distinction between phenomenon and noumena, as, with respect to transcendental idealism, these are the differing conditions for the appropriate placing of particular claims to knowledge. We will thus examine, in this light, the solutions to the dynamical antinomies.

We have already considered the solution to the Third Antinomy above due to its important connection to the *Critique of Practical Reason*. In terms of our present analysis, the causality of freedom is juxtaposed to the causality of nature. The latter necessitates that any being that is to be a cause, must have itself been caused within the horizons of the time-order. The former indicates a 'power of beginning a state spontaneously' (NKS 464). In this way, as a transcendental Idea, freedom does not itself require a cause, nor does its 'object' have a genealogical debt to experience. Spontaneity is a creation of reason which fulfils its desire for a totality where there is only a play of difference. The freedom from sensuous experience is affiliated with the autonomy of practical existence, and both are established through the limitation of the *coercion* of the empirical nexus. Freeing itself from the nexus of empirical causality, the will affirms, contrary to that which has happened, what ought to have happened and what should happen.

Even though the will is implicated in the causality of nature, it can resist this power and its forces through an assertion of a causality of the will. Such a causality, it conceives, may of itself give rise to a new series in the empirical world. Yet this may be, as we have seen, a transgression of the limits of the Idea as it seeks to enter into the empirical world as the intelligible *cause* of a causal series. Does this not make the intelligible cause itself of an empirical character, or at least, taint it to some extent? Is the relation between nature and freedom one of divorcement, the disjunction of an *either/or*, or is it possible to interpret or view 'one and the same event' in differing ways? Kant declares that only if appearances are regarded as things themselves, in the way of homogeneity, is freedom impossible.

If we regard appearances as appearances, as representations, they must have grounds which are not appearances, as presupposed in the expression, *re*-presentation. What is this presence which is *re*-presented? Kant gives his answer to this question of reason, seeking to resolve this conflict of reason with the distinction between the *effects* of the intelligible cause and the *cause itself*, the former being amid the series (necessity), while the latter *acts* outside of the series (freedom). As we will see in the next solution, with respect to the question of necessary being, there is no way an act can not be implicated if it acts as a cause. Yet, in this present case, the will is part and parcel of the series, it is thrown into the empirical nexus of causality. But, the will inhabits two realms at once. It departs from amid the labyrinth of re-presentation, receptivity, yet, there must be a way in which it can be amid this nexus but, at the same time, act in a way which is not only empirically relevant, but can also, through itself, initiate a new series, or, with Foucault, a 'discursive formation'.

How is such a spontaneity possible within the horizons of the phenomenon? The answer is clear and distinct. Just as with the unity of apperception which underlies the acts of the understanding, the causality of the act of reason is the intelligible ground for any event of phenomenality – it is no-thing. Yet, how is this possible? We have already been given a clue in the preceding analysis. From a negative perspective, we can resist sensuous influences – yet, this hides the positive notion of autonomy as the self-determination of the will within the horizons of the interests of reason.

While Jacobi and Hamann, and Heidegger, will refuse the identification of this self-determination with the act of reason itself, we can see that his very assertion of an autonomous self-determining will indicates a sense of freedom which, though departing from the labyrinth, is able to transcend and influence this nexus amid its own positive act of creation which transcends the mere negativity of difference.

As for the fourth conflict of reason, or that of the question of a *necessary being* (dependence of appearances), Kant is not concerned, as he was with the Third Antinomy, with an unconditioned causality, but with the 'unconditioned existence of substance itself' (NKS 479). Moreover, the series that will be the pathway to find the necessary being will not be that of intuitions, but of concepts. That which is sought is the causal derivation of contingent from necessary existence, where the latter need not be a member of the empirical series. The Thesis asserts that such a necessary being is possible, while the Antithesis denies such a being, either in the world or outside the world. Laying out the pathway toward a solution, Kant suggests: 'A way of escape from this apparent antinomy thus lies open to us. Both of the conflicting propositions may be true, if taken in different connections' (NKS 480). These differing connections intimate, in the most obvious way, the distinction between the phenomenon and noumena. Unlike the resolution of the Third Antinomy, the necessary being is not a member of the series, but subsists beyond or before, outside of the nexus of the phenomenon. Indeed, there need be no conflict if we recognise that each assertion is true in the context of its own *topos*. The possibility of such a resolution, in fact a diffusion or dissolution of the conflict, lies, however, in a procedure of limitation of each of the parties to the dispute.

The regulative character of reason is that it can never become constitutive of the empirical object, it is limited with respect to this *topos*. Yet, a theoretical understanding is also limited and must not condemn the Ideas of reason simply due to the fact that they are not susceptible to empirical verification. This latter criterion, on the contrary, is only valid amid the domain to empirical representation. At the same time, empiricism is not the only *topos*, as it is quite *thinkable* that there is an intelligible being which grounds, though does not affect, the *differance* (Derrida) of factical existence. This is not to assert the existence of such a being, which is not what is at issue, as it is only the possibility of such a being that is being conjectured.

It is in this way that Transcendental Idealism, or Critical Philosophy, sets forth powerful answers to the provocation of difficult questions. Kant neither sides with either rationalism or empiricism, nor does he merely destroy each of their deficient assertions. Instead, and the Fourth Antinomy is the perfect example, each party is affirmed, given its own place. Yet, as with the limitation involved in the self-determination of freedom amid the labyrinth of representations, the theoretical and practical each must limit themselves to their own proper domain, as decided via transcendental reflection and codified, archived, in the architectonic of reason. The positive aspect of this situation is that we have been deemed *permitted* not only to understand the real, but also to think the possible. Yet, as we could see through a further reading of the Second *Critique*, this *topos* of the possible is more actual than any reality, as it concerns *lived* existence.

The antinomy of pure reason (cosmology) is the second dialectical inference, or transcendental Idea, after the Paralogisms which concern the soul (psychology), and before the Ideal of Pure Reason which concerns a necessary being (theology). It concerns the world in its significance, as the series and context of involvements, and for Kant, existence is the position (or, perhaps, place, *topos*) amid which the concept and intuition can discretely meet. Yet, reason, as intelligible, can only effect concepts, and in its own pure employment makes use of only those concepts which can grow into Ideas, the object of which is purely intelligible. Beyond the series of the empirical labyrinth lies a transcendental object, which, with respect to the contingency of appearances, is an absolutely necessary being. We will now turn to the exploration of this necessary being in a consideration of the third, and final, dialectical inference of Pure Reason, the Ideal of Pure Reason.

THE IDEAL OF PURE REASON (NKS 485; A567/B595)

An Idea can never be manifest in sensibility since it contains a unity which transcends the contingency of appearance, which can only work for a makeshift unity, an approximation. For Kant, further removed than the Idea is the Ideal, which is regarded not as a particular Idea, but as an individual being, a pure intuition of the Idea as an archetype, from which, as with Plato, the deficiently similar world arises. The Ideal for Kant, unlike Plato, is, however, only regulative, a practical power with regards to the perfectibility of actions.

Kant gives the Stoics as an example, distinguishing the Ideas of Wisdom and Virtue (which give the rule) from the Ideal of the Wise Man (which serves as the archetype). Though such an Ideal, much as with the Ideas, can never attain fulfilment in the empirical order, it is given by reason to serve as a standard, to which we finitely, and incompletely, aspire. Kant contends that the attempt to realise such an Ideal in the world would not only be impractical, but would be absurd since the Idea itself would be disfigured through its association with the world – a contention which could be viewed as an attack on the prophylactics of religion. It is in this connection that he criticises the imagination in that it lacks the rule of conceptual order and discipline, capable only of ideals of sensibility, 'representations such as painters and physiognomists profess to carry in their heads. . .' (NKS 487). Of course, this does not rule out the possibility of the operation of a pure imagination. Yet the point is clear – the ideal will only ever be a vision on the transcendent outer limits of the real.

The Transcendental Ideal (NKS 487; A571/B599)

A concept without determination is empty. It is determined through predication. According to the law of contradiction, only one of two opposing predicates can attach itself to the concept. Contrary to this logical determination with respect to merely two possible predicates, Kant writes that a *thing* is determined by its relationship to every possible predicate. It is not only determined by the law of contradiction, but also by the necessity for a complete determination with respect to the sum of *all* possibilities (sum total of all predicates). From this *transcendental* perspective, the sum of all possibilities could be considered as the *a priori* original source and ground of any individuated, factical thing. In what is a restatement of the principle of individuation,[28] Kant contends that to know a thing, we must compare it to every possible predicate in order to see what it is, for each predicate, however contingent, discloses what the thing is. Once again, such a totality can never be manifest *in concreto*, but remains a regulative Idea of reason. It is itself, as the sum total of all possibility, an Ideal of Pure Reason, signifying the complete determination of an individual being by its Idea (or, with Leibniz, a completely analysed individual).

Kant further distinguishes logical from transcendental philosophy through the examination of negation, a topic made famous in the twentieth century by Heidegger and Carnap. He suggests that logical negation involves the 'not' and 'does not properly refer to a concept, but to its relation to another concept in a judgment' (NKS 489). On the contrary, transcendental negation indicates 'non-being in itself', while transcendental affirmation signifies reality. It is between these two existential possibilities, of non-being and being, that existence, thinghood, is decided. But, with a philosophy that seeks to transcend to the content-filled world, negation can be, for Kant, only derivative vis-à-vis the positive content of reality. And, if this total reality is the substrate of each reality, then negations are, as with our discussion of space, mere limitations to this *a priori* total reality, the unlimited or the All (cf. Anaximander). A thing arises from a limitation of total reality, which is its transcendental condition of possibility. Yet total reality is not only as its ground, but also, in distinction from the universal concept of the logical syllogism, contains the 'thing', as it is the source of each of its predicates.

Logic demands a disjunctive major premise on its way to a determinate conclusion, even though it is blind and ignorant of the kinds of reality upon which it must judge. Transcendental logic is not, however, blind as it traces the relationship between the thing and its condition of possibility, and is oriented by the Ideal as the archetype of all things. This latter possibility of all reality, in distinction from real, synthetic possibilities, is the original condition of all being. This original condition, as the object of the Ideal of Pure Reason, has the tri-partite appellation of 'primordial being' (*ens originarium*), 'highest being' (*ens summum*), and the being of all beings (*ens entium*). Kant warns us that these names pertain only to concepts and not to things, as there can be no knowledge (theoretical, empirical knowledge) of the thing-in-itself. Moreover, correcting his earlier formulations slightly, the supreme being must be thought of as simple, and must not be capable of limitation in the sense of division but must be the ground of being, 'not as their sum'.

Things and our *a priori* modes of determining things follow from the absolutely necessary being as a concrete distillation of all possibility into this possibility, actuality. Yet, things are not contained as actualities in the primordial being, as the barrier between the sensible and the intelligible remains in force. Kant states the obvious that this supreme being is indeed 'God, taken in the transcendental sense. . .' (NKS 493). And, in this light, the Ideal of Pure Reason is the 'object of a transcendental theology' (NKS 493). However, Kant immediately interjects that we have no right to make such an inference to a supreme being in its substantive actuality. For reason, in its regulative employment, is permitted to deploy the transcendental Idea of completion as a 'concept of all reality', but not as a thing which can thus become manifest.

It may be helpful to consider Heidegger's reading of this as a disclosure of human finitude, or the insurmountable impossibility of a knowledge of the totality. From this perspective, it is ironic that the only one who could know the existence of God would be God himself. A further irony is that, for Heidegger, God, as creating what he merely intuits, or imagines, is in no need of a concept, and thus, of knowledge. We travel the ladder from facticity, to the concept, to the Idea, to the Ideal itself, but have neither right nor power to the quite natural conjecture of a supreme being, or to have any knowledge of it at all. Indeed, there is no necessary correlation between the world of sense and that of the intelligible, even though the latter serves as ground for the former.

The difficulty arises when we regard the transcendental condition of the sum of all possibilities as not merely the ground for the empirical realm, but also of all *things in general*. A god arises when this sum of all possibilities is hypostasised into a substantial being. From being the ground for the distributive *topos* of empirical reality, the collective sum of all possibilities, itself, becomes 'God'. But, the *leap* that is being made here is not only a transgression of the horizons of possible experience, it is also a denial of the merely regulative use of the Ideas and Ideals of Pure Reason. We will examine the content of this charge through an examination of Kant's criticisms and refutations of the arguments for the existence of God, those of the ontological, cosmological and the physico-theological proofs.

Speculative Arguments for a Supreme Being (NKS 495; A583/B611)

The ground that is sought by Reason, Kant surmises, will be a resting place from the whirlwind of sensation, understanding, and imagination – from temporal existence. Kant suggests that reason itself will admit that the Ideal is, from the standpoint of the empirical domain, a merely fictitious, vain, but, at the same time, natural, attempt to provide a sufficient foundation for the completion of the series of conditions. Such an unconditioned being can never demonstrate itself in the world, nor could we infer from the concept of such a being that it exists, in that existence is the ground for the synthesis of the understanding, and thus, pertains only to the empirical realm of predicates and relations. At the same time, if we admit the existence of any conditioned being ('it may be, merely, my own existence' [NKS 498]), we will be propelled once again, upon the multi-directional pathway across and through the conditions of the thing, toward the unconditioned.

In this case, Kant is examining the possibility of an absolutely necessary being, as the ground for the totality of the empirical series of existence, even if such a being is incomprehensible. We are driven to the thought, the concept of an *ens realissimum* (the being with the greatest reality, simplicity and unity), which *expresses* the absolutely necessary being, and we cannot be rid of it as it is spawned by the 'natural procedure of human reason' (NKS 497).

For Kant, we need not come to a decision as to the identity of such a supreme being, but may keep the question open as we move along the pathway of philosophical exploration. Yet, another world, or another way of seeing the world, ceaselessly bleeds into the *topos* of the phenomenon. This is the world of practical reason which is given confirmation by the Idea of a supreme being. It is this practical *topos* which compels us to decide in favour of that which, from a theoretical perspective, would be denied any legitimacy or existence. We are compelled to affirm that which we so keenly desire. In this case, it is the unity of the divine, which even, as Kant suggests, polytheists affirm.

There are three pathways, for Kant, in the pursuit of a supreme being. In the first place, we begin with mere concepts and derive the existence of a divinity (ontological proof). In the second place, we begin with existence in general in order derive the foundation of divinity (cosmological proof). In the third place, we begin with the conditioned, seeking the unconditioned which is the 'supreme cause', or, root, of the world (physico-theological proof). In the following, we will examine each of these proofs for the existence of 'God' in light of our preceding excavation, and analysis.

Impossibility of the Ontological Proof (NKS 500; A592/B620)
Kant begins his refutation of the ontological proof with a reflection upon the character of the idea of an absolutely necessary being. Indeed, he asks if in such an idea he is thinking anything, or rather 'nothing at all' (NKS 501). Such a suggestion would, of course, seem to go against the grain of ideological history. Anyone could point out many examples of such a supreme being. And, forms of knowledge could be set forth which exhibit necessity, such as those of mathematics, which could be deployed as proofs for the existence of a being which transcends the horizons of possible experience.

Yet, in light of the merely logical necessity of the idea for reason, such a being, it would seem, will always be arrived at through judgments (conceptual reality). However, Kant declares, 'the unconditioned necessity of judgments is not the same as an absolute necessity of things' (NKS 501). At the end of the day, it is always the thing (actuality) that is required if the truth of a judgment is to be shown in its completeness.

A further difficulty arises in that existence is included in the concept itself, as a way around the *transcendent* status of the idea of a necessary being. Indeed, we could simply reject the idea of a transcendent being with all of its predicates, not simply remaining in the labyrinth of judgments but simply denying the subject and all of its predicates, or as Kant suggests, instead of waxing on the omnipotence of God, we could instead declare, 'There is no God' (NKS 503). There is no contradiction in this statement, until of course we *assent* to the *ontological* proof for the existence of God.

In this argument it is asserted that the concept of the most real being (*ens realissimum*) already must contain the predicate of existence, and therefore, any attempt to deny its existence would be self-contradictory. Kant's refutation of this proof lies in his much acclaimed statement that existence is not a real predicate. In this case, he is contesting the inclusion of the predicate of existence into the concept of a thing which we will only ever be able to admit as a possibility. Such a predication is a mere tautology, as it assumes that which it claims to prove. He declares:

> '*Being*' is obviously not a real predicate; that is, it is not a concept of something which could be added to the concept of a thing. It is merely the positing of a thing, or of certain determinations, as existing in themselves. Logically, it is merely the copula of a judgment. (NKS 504)

The copula merely traces the relation of the subject and the predicate. It does no more, as the concepts involved express real, or merely possible, subjects and predicates. Reality projects the conceptual identity of an object of thought, but has no ability to establish the existence or actuality of the thing. A hundred pounds is the same whether they are merely possible or actual from a logical point of view. But, from the perspective of existence, such a difference would have practical, perhaps dire, significance. Existence adds nothing to a thing in the sense of predication, it merely announces another possibility for thought, and is, as Kant suggests, indistinguishable from possibility.

For us to know the existence of a thing, we must step outside of its concept, and transcend toward the horizons of possible experience, the unity of which is the only domain of the positing of existence. There is only nothing beyond this domain. But, on this criteria, Kant will contend that there is nothing to declare of the actuality or even the possibility of God, and Leibniz's vision of a 'sublime ideal being' was a bit of play by the imagination (empirically conceived; but what of a transcendental imagination that could apprehend existence amid a transcendental, *intellectual intuition*, as with the German Idealists?).

Impossibility of the Cosmological Proof (NKS 507; A603/B631)

The *cosmological* proof begins with existence in general in order to trace a ground in divinity, and it marks itself as distinct from the ontological proof in that it begins with experience. It is similar to that of the ontological in its repertoire of necessity and the highest reality, but argues that the unlimited reality of God is established on the basis of its unconditioned necessity. The argument is as follows:

If anything exists, an absolutely necessary being must also exist.
Now I, at least, exist.
Therefore, an absolutely necessary being exists. (NKS 508)

This argument is distinct from the ontological as it begins with experience, in this case, that of the self. It begins, in the minor premise, already outside of the concept. Yet, not for long, as just as the experience is granted, a leap is made back into the nether regions of transcendent (in distinction from *transcendental*) ideas. Amid this *topos*, as God could not be found in the world, his properties are defined by reason, and he is described as the most real being.

However, for Kant, there is no way back to the world once the horizons of possible experience have been transgressed. Existence, once again (but in a poorly disguised form), is not a real predicate, and cannot be derived from the concept of the highest reality. In this light, the most necessary being remains an idea born of a needful dialectic of reason, which however wondrous its intellectual creations, can never assert, with certainty, the existence of such a supreme condition.

Impossibility of the Physico-Theological Proof (NKS 518; A620/B6648)

The *physico-theological* proof of the existence of God begins with the conditioned, in the 'present world', and the intricate and sublime order of things – and seeks the unconditioned which is the supreme root, or substance, of the world. Kant examines this apparent need for a supreme condition for the sublime event of existence:

Nothing has of itself come into the condition in which we find it to exist, but always points to something else as its cause, while this in turn commits us to repetition of the same enquiry. The whole universe must thus sink into the abyss of nothingness, unless, over and above this infinite chain of contingencies, we assume something to support it. (NKS 519)

Yet, in keeping with his *Inaugural Dissertation*, and its echoes in the Transcendental Dialectic, Kant forbids any possible contiguity between the sensible and intelligible worlds, and thus denies any affirmation of a divinity on the basis of experience – the 'wonders of nature' or the 'majesty of the universe' in the present world. Again we are invited to ascend the staircase of conditions to the unconditioned.

Everywhere we see signs of God, everything has been designed for its purpose by God, this being is the sublime, intelligent and free cause and we can see his effects in the order of the world. God is the artist of nature. However, again, such a proof cannot be certain for, as it has not found God in nature, it can rely in the first instance only upon the analogy between human and divine art, and with the failure of such an analogical connection, it can only fall back upon the ontological proof (from concepts to existence), one which, as we have already seen, Kant declares as one of our most evident human errors, and thus, a primary, root-concept in the self-criticism of pure reason. He states that we must admire this oldest proof of the existence of God, but must refuse to it an assent with respect to certainty.

Critique of All Theology (NKS 525; A631/B659)
We begin in the world as conditioned and contingent, we seek out conditions for our existence. However, that which conditions us is only relatively greater than ourselves, not absolute but 'needful' (NKS 527). The speculative procedure of positing an object for its concept has existential limits. It cannot be deployed by reason in its attempt to find a being which fulfils its concept, its intention. No synthetic proposition can be admitted that transcends the horizons of possible experience, of nature (unless there be a transcendental imagination and/or intellectual intuition, which Kant suppresses between the A and B editions, in the former case, and denies with respect to the latter). Indeed, the concept of causality can only be applied within the empirical domain, to appearances, and any transcendent use is invalid.

Returning implicitly to the distinction between phenomenon and noumenon, Kant indicates the difference in perspective with respect to practical reason. In this aspect of reason, there is no need for a theoretical determination of an object. Practical reason is concerned with the Moral Law (cf. the Second *Critique*), and would admit the existence of a god (in *Religion within the Limits of Reason Alone*, he includes the pagan gods and Allah) as a postulate, which supports a moral law which is at once conditioned and necessary. There is no way to step beyond the immanence of reason amid its ideation. And, in this light, the gods of this world are conditioned, empirical, but do not have the overwhelming attributes of the Judeo-Christian-Islamic God, which is the real target here in its physico-theological, onto-theological, cosmo-theological manifestations. Such speculative pursuits of God are, for Kant, 'fruitless' and 'null and void', as the very possibility of any *actual* object is denied in advance. However, Kant's criticisms of theology concern those *types* which are based upon speculative reason, conceived as a speculum that creates its own object and seeks to find and/or invent such an object to satisfy its own needs.

Yet, Kant does not thereby throw the baby out with the bathwater, for, as we have seen, there is not only a powerful practical significance to the idea of God, there is also much strength in its existence as an ideal standard for projects amid the contingent, finite world. He declares that, although it can never be known, the ideal of God is an 'ideal without a flaw, a concept which completes and crowns the whole of human knowledge' (NKS 531). In contrast to the speculative theologies which seek an object, Kant suggests a transcendental theology as a framework for a practical faith in respect of the moral law.

Such a practical theology is not contradicted by theoretical reason, but as it respects the limits of the aspects of reason, it can assert itself upon its own *topos*, in this case, the practical domain of the Will. However, with respect only to the First *Critique*, such a transcendental theology would serve only a negative role as an absolute limitation of speculative theologies from the island of strict, universal and necessary knowledge (within the unity of experience).

On the Regulative Employment of the Ideas (NKS 532; A643/B671)

Sounding much like Jacobi, Kant flatters the sound knowledge of the empirical understanding over against the delusions of reason. Yet, he also acknowledges that the seduction of the flights of reason are irresistible. This is our double-bind: we desire answers to questions for which there are no answers. Of course, this double-bind is *ultimate* as we are finite beings, and will never know *what* we seek. Yet, there are other ways of seeing things, and of conceiving the contours and limitations of our existence in light of the double-bind.

Kant supposes that each of our powers may have some appropriate employment suited to it, and that this may be the case as well with the Ideas of reason. That which suits reason is to direct itself to the 'understanding and its effective application' (NKS 533). He sets forth an analogy: the Ideas of reason order the concepts of the understanding just as the latter orders appearances. Yet, what is different is that reason drives the understanding to seek totality in each and all of its myriad series, even if such pursuits entail a transgression of the horizons of possible experience.

If we are aware of and limit the fallacious deployments of the Ideas, however, and apprehend their regulative significance, we can use these concepts in order to 'direct the understanding toward a certain goal. . .' (NKS 533). It is interesting that Kant casually writes that the convergence of the idea and the concept is a *focus imaginarius*, an imaginary point, lying outside the horizons of the empirical domain, of sense, reproductive imagination and understanding, for that may seem to imply a transcendental imagination, working with or *as reason itself*. Yet, reason, in its logical aspect, once again, prescribes a unity of knowledge as a principle of the subsumption of the particular under a universal 'in a necessary manner'. It seeks a 'systematic unity of the knowledge of the understanding', (NKS 535) with its own rule-structure as the criterion of truth. Yet, as regulative, the unity of the system is to be regarded as problematic, and as merely a temporal, existential projection.

Jacobi and Hamann can be glimpsed in the background of this radical limitation of reason from its earlier rationalist and analytic pretensions (we can see echoes of these pretensions in the logical positivist 'revolution', which has long been rejected by analytic philosophers, especially by those of either a historical perspective or those of the *later* Wittgenstein persuasion). At the end of the day, the Ideas of reason, for Kant, *become* merely regulative, with respect to the domain of the *sciences*. This limitation of itself in one respect is in another respect a great liberation, since upon the practical *topos*, it can directly determine the Will and command respect for the moral law, for the *practical* concerns of truth – regardless of the (theoretically determined) empirical considerations.

The Natural Dialectic of Human Reason (NKS 549; A669/B697)
The purpose of the Ideas of reason is to give systematic unity to the operations of the understanding, and thus, in a mediate, schematic way, to be the source and ground of the unity of objects. From a transcendental perspective, Kant contends that this character of

ground and source for the unity of the object serves as a deduction of the concepts of reason in their heuristic, regulative employment.

Kant cautions all who do not consent to his transcendental distinctions between theoretical, speculative and practical deployments of reason, each of which has its own appropriate 'object'. He seeks to negotiate a way among the differing perspectives, of theoretical, transcendent, realist objectifications toward a *topos* of existence, as a place where sense and concept emerge together from a common root, as if from a dream of the imagination, or of the subconscious of Schelling. There is 'something', some 'power' that drives us on, seduces us to the abyss of the question, and onto the chaotic terrain of disparate answers, of assertions and counter-assertions. It is not a being, a substance – but it must be the ground of beings.

It is this situation that expresses the internal conflict of reason with itself, of the 'natural dialectic of reason', a conflict which is its basic state, one which denies the unity which it craves. Kant's solution seems to be that of a philosophy of the *as if*. We admit that there is nothing we can know of the ideas, but we also seek to put the ideas to use for our 'best advantage', in a regulative manner. There can be no theoretical knowledge of the soul, of a simple substance (monad), but we proceed and act *as if* this were the case. We could never experience a never-ending series in the empirical realm, but we proceed *as if* there is such an infinity. We further proceed as if experience were an absolute unity and that beyond its limits lay its intelligible ground in a 'self-subsistent, original, creative reason' (NKS 551). We assume that each thing contains the traces of the archetype of reason; or, in other words, we presume the intelligibility of the world, but acknowledge that reason may only regulate the understanding and never manifest its own idols in the world.

Once again, it is interesting that the Idea of reason bestows itself to the concepts of the understanding through a schema, a product of the transcendental imagination. This possibility should be kept in mind if a critical and hermeneutical understanding of the First *Critique*, in both of its Editions, is to be achieved. It is in these ambiguities, as I have suggested, that there is a susceptibility of criticism or of a radical re-interpretation enacted first by the German Idealists, and later, in his own way, by Heidegger. One could suggest, in this light, that reason could not exercise its regulative role if it did not have the capacity for an *a priori* synthesis of a regulative schema. Since synthesis is the product of imagination, the inclusion of imagination in a 'creative' reason would seem to be a necessary conclusion. Yet, such a possibility, while seemingly unavoidable, is, at the same time, impossible.

An inclusion of imagination, even one that was *a priori* and transcendental, would infect the eternity of reason with temporality. Not only would the transcendental distinction between sensibility and intelligibility break down, but the ideas, in their current figuration as substantial forms, would also collapse. The question would then arise as to a possible temporal source of conceptuality in the schematisations of the transcendental imagination, which for Heidegger is another word for temporality. This was also a question raised by Hegel, and his own variation of an inclusion of imagination within reason (or an identification of the two) gave rise to the specific temporal character of his philosophy.

Yet, for Kant, such an inclusion cannot be admitted as it would deny to him, as Cassirer testifies, the object of his desires which was eternity. Moreover, such an inclusion is already excluded on the basis of the whole strategy of the Second *Critique*, in its *practical* resuscitation of all those substantial forms which Kant had previously destroyed and eliminated. The imagination could, in such a restrictive scenario, figure as merely a 'title' for an act of the understanding as in the B Deduction. Yet, the question does not seem to be raised with respect to reason in all of its creative acts. Kant disparages the images of the painters et al., but he does not consider an *a priori*, transcendental employment of imagination, except in his denial of *intellectual intuition*, although there are myriad traces of the acts and influences of imagination in the regulative employment of reason.

Perhaps this difficult question is never pursued since reason is only to have a regulative employment, and as it is not constitutive, the question of its power of manifestation of an object is never raised, nor on Kant's terms, could it ever be raised. Yet, as reason is forever seeking the ends in all things, such a question is still raised, but as a transgression of Kant's architectonic.

Having now completed our reading of Division One of the First *Critique*, we will now begin a more restricted investigation of Kant's methodological system in the dramatically shorter Transcendental Doctrine of Method. In the next chapter, we will describe each of the four divisions of Kant's doctrine of method, articulated as the Discipline, Canon, Architectonic, and History *of pure reason*.

Study questions

1. What are the argumentative similarities and differences between the paralogisms, antinomies and the refutations of the existence of God?
2. What is the source of the 'natural dialectic of reason' for Kant? What is the role of the imagination in the operations of reason?

TRANSCENDENTAL DOCTRINE OF METHOD (NKS 571; A705/B733)

Kant compares his philosophical efforts to that of building a 'dwelling house' amid experience, and not a tower into the sky. In our previous readings, we have already witnessed the demolition of the tower, in the wake of its pretensions to touch the sky, the face of God. Indeed, the success of this tower was limited by its lack of materials and by the 'babel of tongues' (NKS 573), of those who, in the battles of metaphysics, spun conflict as their raison d'être. Nothing built on so shifting an edifice could ever survive. Such nihilism will never compare to the relative stability of our dwelling house, our makeshift *topos*.

Yet, even this modest dwelling has a building plan, one that is cognate with our horizons of limitation, and which serves our 'best advantage'. The doctrine of method lays out the 'formal condition of a complete system of pure reason' (NKS 573). This is not the system itself, we should add, and it would be appropriate to compare the formal conditions of Kant with the attempts by the German Idealists and even Materialists to build such towers into the sky (or to destroy these towers).

Such towers will always be brought back down to earth, back to this *topos* from which we always begin – and then again, they will again arise in an eternal recurrence of the same. We are aware that it is the character of reason to seek the All, but there is *at the same time* an aspect of reason which sets out a limitation to its own self – a self-determination that is the basis for the autonomy of the practical self amid the *kingdom of ends*. Kant does not deny the eternal recurrence of tragic existence, but takes a step back into an autonomy of self-determination which allows him to disclose the *practical*, ethical significance of existence.

All that we have read and thought about in the previous pages is now to be projected as an organisational plan for knowledge, thought, Being and becoming. This fourfold plan is echoed in Schopenhauer's *Fourfold Root of the Principle of Sufficient Reason*, published nine years after Kant died, in which he criticises the limitation of the Will to mere thought and a direct determination by reason. We will return to this point after a detour into transcendental method.

The Discipline of Pure Reason (NKS 574; A709/B737)

The discipline Kant seeks to establish is that of a negative knowing – a haunting critical shadow of knowing that acknowledges its own *non-knowing* (cf. Bataille, *Inner Experience*) distinct from the *Canon of Pure Reason*, which is concerned with a positive *topos* of praxis, of action and will (*eros*). The discipline of pure reason is a methodology of criticism, which has for its object an extensive network of errors and illusions, generated by pure reason. And, again, the archive of rational knowledge will be divided by the phenomenon of reason itself in its errancy.

The discipline will thus have as its divisions its various employments, in this case, those of the dogmatic, polemical and hypothetical.

With its dogmatic employment, reason acknowledges its limitations as a discursive concept of things in general (philosophy), in distinction to mathematics, which in its definitions, axioms and demonstrations operates with the construction of a concept via *a priori* intuition, time and space. As we have seen over the last chapters, Kant is seeking to limit the employment of reason to the horizons of possible experience. Indeed, he contends, 'it is precisely in knowing its limits that philosophy consists' (NKS 585). Yet, in this way, Kant argues that the discipline that would curtail reason to its own limits would neither be dogmatic, as a judgment (synthetic *a priori* propositions) derived from concepts, nor mathematical (in the constructions of concepts). As there are no synthetic *a priori* propositions in speculative reason, it makes no judgments of this sort, but respects the horizons of possible experience and acts to regulate the employment of understanding.

In its polemical employment, discipline has the meaning of unfolding a legal order to arbitrate the disputations of reason which are inevitable. Kant advocates widespread freedom of criticism, but establishes the autonomy of the transcendental philosopher as the arbiter and examiner who is not party to the dispute of reason with itself. He is already intimating his Canon as that domain of faith which may extricate itself from the war of ideas. And, while encouraging the exercise of free rational thought, he begins to promote the greater significance of the practical domain and the practical employment of the Ideas of reason. He asks, 'For how can two persons carry on a dispute about a thing the reality of which neither of them can present in actual or even in possible experience. . .' (NKS 601).

Once again, it is the transgressions of its limits which brings about the appearance of a polemic or antinomy of reason. But, from the perspective of the transcendental critic, the polemic is merely a generational dispute in the activity of reason itself between the tendencies toward dogmatism (infancy) and scepticism (childhood). Criticism however is reason in its maturity as it, guided by the Idea of unity, has transcended the state of nature through respect for the Moral Law.

The Law is not designed to censor reason and its 'facts', but to determine its limits within the context of its own self-legislation. The concepts of reason are to be regarded as *a priori* principles, such as that of causality, which 'anticipate experience'. This principle (a concepts appropriated by reason) does not merely report that which has occurred and make a prediction in the manner of Hume. Instead, the concept, while emerging perhaps from the empirical event, becomes, through reflection, associated no longer with an actual experience, but with a possible experience. It thereby becomes transcendental as it could then apply to any experience, but only in a regulative manner.

In its hypothetical employment, discipline is an attempt to further disclose the limits of reason, in this case, as a prohibition on the creation of additional faculties, for instance, an understanding which could intuit it own objects out of experience. Indeed, while the practice of creating hypotheses is a necessary activity in science (in the empirical order), its use in the context of reason must be limited to the domain of possible experience. There can be no transcendental hypotheses which would establish the truth of substance or of God, for instance.

If we did not criticise this use of hypotheses, the antithetical battle would reignite on a differing basis, not this time on the basis of assertions, but upon the tenuousness of hypotheticals, which are always problematic. Again, reason reveals the limitations for its own activity as those of possible experience, in which a previously visionary imagination is set to work, 'inventive under the strict surveillance of reason' (NKS 613).

In the wake of the discipline, the limits of pure reason are disclosed, not only as the critical limitation of its legitimate truth character, but also with regards to its regulative employment in the empirical domain. Not only does reason work to make the sensible world 'systematically coherent' (NKS 623), it also serves as the transcendental condition of possibility of the sensible world. But it is at this limit that we must stop. We may rightly infer and prove the necessity of a transcendental condition in the sense of the concept of causality, for instance. Yet, we are not to attempt to reveal causality as such as an object in the world (or to build 'other-worldly' kingdoms ruled by an infinite cause), but to reflect upon the necessity of this concept for there to be any experience of a dynamical character in the first place.

At the same time, what seems to be of greater interest to Kant is the practical employment of reason which is never subject to the dialectic of theoretical reason. Beyond being the administrator of the understanding, and the transcendental ground of the world, reason has a positive employment upon its own proper territory. From the theoretical perspective, reason stands as archetype, limit and ground, but only in the form of regulative Ideas. In the practical realm, reason acts directly without the necessity of limiting itself from the empirical domain. In this light, we will turn to the second part of the transcendental doctrine of method, 'The Canon of Pure Reason', so as to explore this practical employment of reason in more depth.

The Canon of Pure Reason (NKS 630; A797/B825)

In the first instance, with the intervention of critical philosophy, reason is at first humiliated by its former pretensions. It then becomes oriented to its new status as the practitioner of its own discipline, and as a critic scrutinises assertions which claim to have the character of truth. Yet, in addition to its negative role, Kant states that there must be some positive mode of knowledge associated with pure reason, not certainly in the speculative realm, but in regard to practical employment. In this light, the canon of pure reason is the totality of principles for the proper exercise of this faculty in the practical realm. We can see that Kant is beginning to leave the First *Critique* behind as he states that this canon is not that of a speculative reason, as this latter can only be negative in light of the impossibility of it having its own object (there is no synthetic knowledge through reason). The canon is that of reason in its practical employment, in fact, a canon of practical reason, which is now clearly autonomous from theoretical, speculative reason.

Kant re-evaluates the drive of reason for totality and the unconditioned – its pure employment, but not with respect to the limits of theoretical reason, rather with respect to the interests of practical reason. Indeed, from this perspective the drive of reason to the unconditioned may be reinterpreted in terms of the intentionality of reason with respect to its ends and aims. Kant states that, in the horizons of the practical interests of reason, the ultimate aim of reason is described by three objects: freedom of the will, immortality of the soul and the existence of God.

These objects, as we have seen, are irrelevant to speculative knowledge, and have, for Kant, a practical significance, where practical indicates 'everything that is possible through freedom' (NKS 632). Such an employment of reason is not limited by the empirical realm, as is the case with the regulative use of reason, but in a freedom from any pragmatic restriction of reason in the recognition of laws which are *a priori* and absolute. Such laws, for Kant, are moral laws which 'belong to the practical employment of reason' (NKS 632). Kant divides the canon of pure reason along the lines of the ultimate aim and its three objects – but taken in the practical sense of action. He asks, 'what we ought to do, if the will is free, if there is a God and a future world' (NKS 632). Practical reason, not concerned with what is, but with what ought to be, sets forth laws which are 'imperatives, that is, objective laws of freedom', 'practical laws' (NKS 634). Reason cultivates and enforces its autonomy from the influences of sensibility in its state of transcendental freedom.

While such freedom will remain problematic from a speculative perspective, with regard to the practical domain, it is freedom itself which is the basis of the practical and its acts, and thus, its question is answered. The two remaining questions, however, still express an unresolved crisis of reason: 'Is there a God? and, Is there a future life' (NKS 634).

In pursuit of the Ideal of the highest good, Kant asks three more questions: What can I know? What ought I to do? What may I hope? The first question is answered simply (theroretically): in respect to the existence of God and of a future life, we can know nothing. The second question is merely moral, and the third is moral and the-oretical, and is concerned, Kant writes, with happiness. Reason is always already concerned with the world in a practical way and making demands, and is a condition of possible experience in the sense of the historicity of moral existence – or as a new way to see the world, in its practical meaning.

But, while Kant will admit the traces of reason in history and in the various pursuits of happiness (and our worthiness of happiness through good conduct), he will contend that there is a moral law which is *a priori* and that true morality is not thereby instituted with respect to empirical motives, but as the aspects and laws of a moral world. This world is merely intelligible (for what is remains distinct from what ought to be), and is thus a mere idea. But, with the new power of the practical, such an idea may affect the world and seek to bring it into the image of the idea.

Practical reason is a different way of seeing and acting in the world, one not of means and unfree wills, but of a *corpus mysticum* of rational beings. The question of happiness and of its involvement in morality, in the question 'what ought I do?', leads to the further question of what secures this happiness, the ideal of the supreme good, the ground of a moral world, the postulate of God. And as the connection between moral worth and happiness cannot be demonstrated in the field of sensibility, there is postulated further a future life which is linked to our conduct in the world of sense. None of this is indeed necessary for Kant, yet, as our kingdom of ends exists in the world of means, morality as a system of commands, must, from a practical perspective, be grounded in reward and pun-ishment of supreme being, the highest good and the transcendental condition for any 'purposive unity'. Maxims are practical laws which serve as the 'subjective grounds of actions' (NKS 640). These maxims are necessary, and they must be connected to the moral law. It is not happiness that is the goal of morality, unless this be con-nected to the moral law, and thus, would be complete happiness. The postulation of a God as the ground of the universal order of things is required by the unity of ends, and this, Kant writes, must have the attributes of the traditional deity, omniscience, omnipo-tence, and omni-presence. The perfection of the supreme being becomes the principle of unity and may in turn influence the other deployments of unity (or lead to looking at the other deploy-ments in a different way), as in the case of the search for ends in the theoretical perspective, a search illuminated through the regulative idea of purposiveness in nature, a topic to which Kant would return in the Third *Critique*.

At the end of the day, what the canon implies, as in Nietzsche's aphorism 'Kant's Joke', is that the greatest mind knows nothing more than the ordinary mind, but only perhaps has a greater degree of sophistication in the admission that he knows nothing.

The Architectonic of Pure Reason (NKS 653; A832/B860)

Architectonic is the 'art of constructing systems' (NKS 653). It is also the study of the scientific character of our knowledge as it is grounded in a systematic unity. Kant writes, 'By a system I understand the unity of the manifold modes of knowledge under one idea' (NKS 653). Kant likens a system to the totality of an organism, which is not to be conceived as a mere aggregate. The idea realises itself through a schema, and achieves technical unity if its schema is that of the empirical imagination, and an architectonic unity if it 'propounds the end *a priori*, and does not wait for them to be empirically given' (NKS 654). Each system is based upon an idea, and each system is united with every other in their emergence from the self-development of reason, as a great 'system of human knowledge' (NKS 655).

Kant mentions the Idea of a common root of our faculty of understanding, one of the stems being reason, but does not seek to begin the construction of a system himself, limiting his task to an outline of the architectonic. I have given his outline as flow chart, together with a discussion.

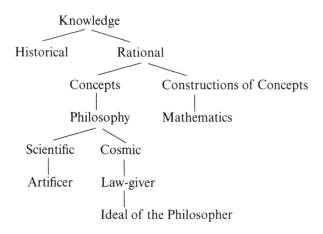

The Philosopher is concerned with the essential ends of human reason, and its highest end, the ultimate end. All other ends serve the ultimate end as means. Kant declares that the ultimate end is the vocation of man and this end, this calling, is the object of moral philosophy. The Philosopher is regarded as the law-giver of human reason, and this legislation concerns the domains of nature and freedom, of the laws of nature and moral laws, respectively. The ultimate goal of the philosopher is to present these stems, the *is* and the *ought* of knowledge, in one system.

Again, Kant does not plan to do this here. And, until that time, we are left with the divisions of our knowledge, and of the various regions of inquiry (which would continue to thrive even if a system was not forthcoming). There are pure reason, empirical principles, criticism and metaphysics, which in turn are divided into speculative and practical, or between a metaphysics of nature (theoretical knowledge) and a metaphysics of morals (moral actions). Indeed, it is the task of the philosopher to lay out the entire tapestry of human knowledge, drawing up its limits and relations, *a priori* and *a posteriori*.

But, for Kant, it is necessary for the philosopher to turn to his own house and make sure that it is in order. He is indeed setting forth a new metaphysics or metaphysical method, united to the critical method, which is guided by the rational demand for systematic unity. It is from this citadel of systematic unity that we may begin to trace the genealogies of the various stems of knowledge, such as speculative knowledge and practical reason.

Kant divides his proposed new system of metaphysics into four parts: ontology, rational psychology, rational cosmology and rational theology. The four divisions are parts of a systematic whole which is grounded in the idea of a philosophy of pure reason. The organisation of the elements of the system is an illustration of the architectonic of pure reason, in its own critical self-exposition. As we can see, the architectonic places into systematic unity all of the insights of the lengthy explorations we have encountered in our reading. The central attempt of this architectonic is, Kant admits, to bring about harmony through not only respect for limits, but also through the criticism of those ideologies which lose sight of the 'supreme end, the happiness of all mankind' (NKS 665).

The History of Pure Reason (NKS 666; A852/B880)

Kant gives a very short history of pure reason, indeed, as a project which 'future workers must complete'. He limits himself to giving a brief sketch of the 'chief revolutions [in metaphysical theory]' (NKS 667). The first, tied to the names of Epicurus and Plato, concerned the status of the object. The former was a sensualist, the latter an intellectualist, intimating Kant's own concern with empiricism and rationalism. The second, tied to Aristotle and Plato (and their respective heirs Locke and Leibniz), concerns the origin of ideas, and of the opposing empiricist and rationalist explanations. The third concerns the method of philosophy and the primacy of principles, which may be naturalistic or scientific. The former leads to 'misology', the hatred of logic, while the latter is a pathway which has been populated for the history of pure reason by dogmatism (Wolff) and scepticism (Hume). Kant does not seek to destroy these positions, but insists that they should 'proceed systematically' (NKS 668). Yet, he announces that there is another pathway, that of the critical, which 'alone is still open'. And it is the goal of this revolution, Kant's own, which seeks to achieve a secure *topos* for human knowledge through the critical self-exposition of reason.

Study questions

1. What is the Discipline of Pure Reason? What is its role in the practice of Critical Philosophy?
2. Can there truly be a history of pure reason in light of the latter's lack of a relation with time? If so, in what sense does reason undergo historical change?

EPILOGUE: THE *CRITIQUE OF PURE REASON*

We have now completed our reading of the *Critique of Pure Reason*, and are probably left with more questions than we began with. Kant's Critical Philosophy, or Transcendental Idealism, required such a strict limitation of our knowledge, or pretensions to knowledge, that all was left in confusion in his wake. The First *Critique* is the first projection in Kant's radical reorganisation and reorientation of knowledge and its method. We can see that it contains the seeds of the later *Critiques*, yet, it must be interpreted not only within the horizons of its own limitations of questioning, but also in regard to its status as a contested text. Whether or not we agree with the minutae of Kant's reasonings and examples, it is clear that he has set forth an ambitious attempt to come to terms with some of the most difficult questions of human knowledge, questions (together with his solutions) that are still with us.

We have not merely adopted Kant hook, line and sinker, but have merely recognised his substantial influence on the lexicon, methodology and practice of philosophy of the current era. Indeed, his philosophy is already rich in controversy, ambiguity and error, and it is precisely in such richness, that the fertility of philosophy is revealed. We would never expect a single person to think for us, to lay down the law for all time, nor would we desire such a tyranny. But, Kant has crucially altered the landscape of our philosophical questioning and this is why we have attempted to come to terms with his philosophy. In the final chapter, we will lay out the dominant receptions of the *Critique of Pure Reason*. Though the account will be by no means exhaustive, I will try to describe some of the most significant influences of and disputes arising from Kant's work.

Study questions

1. Is it accurate to suggest that Kant's transcendental philosophy contains within itself an uneasy, though seemingly durable, compromise between rationalism and empiricism?
2. Why is it necessary for Kant to limit knowledge to make room for faith? In what sense are we free from theoretical considerations in the domain of practical reason?

CHAPTER 4

RECEPTION AND INFLUENCE

There were many receptions of the *Critique of Pure Reason* imme-diately following its initial publication in 1781. This is a complex history, even in terms of the subsequent transformation of the text itself in its Second Edition of 1787, and would require a separate book of its own. In the following, and knowing my limits, I will schematically lay out the major receptions of the First *Critique*, ending with a prospective sketch of the current state of philosophy and the recurrent significance of Kant and the post-Kantians.

THE RATIONALISTS

We have already explored the relationship of rationalism to the *Critique of Pure Reason* throughout most of this Reader's Guide. We have already heard the echoes of the condemnation by rationalists such as Mendelssohn who claimed that Kant had 'destroyed every-thing'. Yet, we have also heard the simultaneous positive responses by empiricists and anti-rationalist religious philosophers, such as Hamann and Jacobi, and romantics such as Schiller and Goethe. While we will consider these latter in more detail in the next section, in this section we must consider the rationalist perspective in order to comprehend its horror in the face of the First *Critique*. In essence, Kant took from rationalism its universal project of reason, not only with respect to the certainty and nature of its concepts, but also its moral universe of substantial forms and entities (its great artwork). Not only was Kant dangerously flirting with solipsism and subjective idealism (in a Berkeleyan sense), but he had unhinged the authority of reason to such an extent as to make it untenable. The criterion of the horizons of possible experience denies any theoretical power to reason – and the consolation of a proactive practical reason with its mere postulates is no satisfaction to the interests of reason. That which is threatened is the unity of reason itself.

Of course, Kant spent much time battling these criticisms in his *Prolegomena* and in his reworking of the *Critique* for the Second Edition. Indeed, these criticisms were a significant influence upon the recasting and diminishment by Kant of the role of a pure imagination in the constitution of knowledge (indeed, some would argue that imagination would have been better placed in a theology than in an immanent criticism of pure reason). It is obvious that Kant's revisions have left much ambiguity in the *Critique*. However, it is also clear that Kant, as Beiser notes, in the context of the 'Pantheism controversy' came down on the side of Mendelssohn to the dismay of the empiricists and romantics who had looked either to Kant's radical criticism of pure reason or to his doctrine of imagination. We will now turn to this other reception.

THE 'PANTHEISM' CONTROVERSY

The 'Pantheism Controversy', as we have seen, was a philosophical dispute instigated by Jacobi in his attack on Lessing for his 'Spinozism.' At the time, this charge, in its characterisation of rationality as nihilistic, was tantamount to one of 'atheism'. Indeed, some time after this particular controversy, Jacobi would turn his sights on Fichte's alleged atheism. However, in this dispute, the question was that of the *authority* of reason. Jacobi, like his ally Hamann, was a religious empiricist who put great significance upon the notion of faith and the fundamental role of imagination in knowledge. After the appearance of the First Edition of the *Critique of Pure Reason*, Jacobi felt sure that Kant had come down on the side of his way of thinking. Indeed, was not a criticism of pure reason a contestation of its power and authority? Moreover, had not Kant spoken of limiting knowledge to make room for faith? And, finally, had not Kant given a tremendous amount of significance to the imagination and its creative and synthetic roles in the constitution of finite knowledge? Yet, with the publication of the Second Edition of the *Critique*, Jacobi and his allies became convinced of a drastic shift in perspective on the part of Kant. The authority of reason was reasserted in proportion to the diminishment of the power of imagination, they alleged. And it is significant that Kant continued to assert the rational limits and horizons of imagination not only in his other works of the period, but also in his subsequent critical examinations.

Yet, the deeper issue is not merely one of rationalism versus empiricism, but of the status of imagination, and hence, religion, faith, or even a phenomenological openness to the world, in relation to reason and its omnivorous apperception. Both Hamann and Jacobi were opponents of the authority of reason, and each approached this opposition from a religious (Christian) perspective, with emphasis upon tradition (custom, history), faith or a belief either in 'God' or in the phenomenon of the senses, which cannot be demonstrated by reasons, but can only be apprehended. It is the imagination which is the terrain of such a perspective, as it opens out into the world, transcending over toward the world of objects, as a knowledge, or even a wisdom, of the practical world of life. It is this perspective which Kant must displace if he is to secure the authority of reason *over the imagination*, or as Kant describes it in a formula: 'Religion within the Limits of Reason Alone'. It is this sense of the *a priori*, that of mere existence, which relies not upon logic or reason, either being indifferent to it, as Hamann was – advocating creation, submission to God, and sensuality – or hostile to it, as with Jacobi, who invited his reader to take a mortal leap into the abyss of 'faith'. Each of these thinkers was not opposed to reason for mere intellectual *reasons*, but charged that reason, in its universalist pretensions, was subversive of practical wisdom and order, of the situation and perspective of morality and religion, and even of ethics.

Their response to this threat was an exclusion of reason as such from the domain of essential knowledge. All philosophy was practical philosophy, which in this case, meant that philosophy was indistinguishable from some form of imaginative apprehension of the world, 'faith' in its broadest sense. It is reason which leads to a destruction of belief, and hence, of the root of knowledge in the imagination. In his own way, and as we have seen in our treatment of the Second *Critique*, Kant acknowledges the incompatibility of theoretical reason with the domain of practical wisdom, but instead of giving to imagination this domain for its own concern, as the field of its principal operation (as it would be if it were a primary faculty of knowledge), Kant contains the imagination in a 'subsumptive' relationship with respect to the understanding, and divides reason into two spheres of influence and grounding, theoretical reason and practical reason. Via this containment of imagination, Kant saves the authority *and the purity* of reason, and gives to the practical a relative autonomy with respect to *theoretical* reason.

If we read only Kant's text, the so called 'jugglers', such as Jacobi – whom he calls men of genius, or perhaps, apes of genius – would be lost in his meta-philosophical myth of the 'battleground of metaphysics', the 'queen of the sciences', of the 'combat between dogmatism and scepticism', 'enthusiasts', etc. Without the appeal of other voices, we are compelled to accept Kant's audacious claim that no further philosophical work would ever be required with regard to his conceptual apparatus, only its ceaseless application. However, to the extent that Kant is seeking to defend the authority of reason and the autonomy of logic, from the world, from intuition and imagination, to the extent that he identifies knowledge with judgment, and thus places it within the horizons of logical-conceptual determination, he is indeed 'correct' within his own sphere of philosophical concerns.

For Kant is presenting an answer to the question: how are synthetic *a priori* judgments possible? It is the word 'judgment' which makes his exposition of the theme consistent with respect to his original definitions and presuppositions, and with the goal of his inquiry. Of course, this is not to suggest that Kant has succeeded, but merely to distinguish him from his contemporaries, those who were the constituent voices in a broader dialogue. Moreover, and in light of Heidegger's destruction of the Kantian imagination, we can ask – even or especially if Kant succeeds on his own terms, which seems a problematic claim – whether his notion of a logical and conceptual *a priori* be the last and only word in the halls of philosophy. Or, more directly, whether such a grounding of knowledge can be sustained if, in its Platonistic severance from the domains of sensibility and imagination, reason and its inexorable application leads, as Jacobi warned, to 'nihilism'.

We have intimated that there exist other ways to an *a priori*, but, as for Hamann and Jacobi, and for Heidegger as well, to an *a priori* which does not rely on the logic of identity or upon a sovereignty of apperception which was the alpha and omega of transcendental philosophy with its postulate of the authority of reason. The price of this authority is the subjection of the power of imagination and, one might suggest, a debasement of the 'worldly philosophers'. Yet some – for instance, Hamann – were not willing to pay this price, which was like contracting a hitman to kill oneself.

Hamann, for his part, in his short essay 'Metakritik of the "Purism" of Pure Reason',[29] called Kant, with his assertion of the authority of reason, 'blind', a 'sleepwalker', lost in the artificial constructions of reason, and advocated instead 'setting free' the spontaneity of imagination amidst this opening of the world, in which he saw the myriad symbolism of God as such, a symbolism to which his response, in a manner a great distance from that of Kant, was to write poetic rhapsodies, holding on to his own nothingness in the face of the divine. In this light, it is hardly surprising that it was Hamann who, having been the first to read the *Critique of Pure Reason*, suggested that it was imagination which was the 'common root' for understanding and sensibility. It was toward the question of the sources of knowledge in existence that Hamann oriented his probing of the symbolism of the divine.

Beiser remarks that Kant, in his essay, 'What is Orientation in Thinking?' written in 1786, published one year before the B Edition, makes a definite break with Hamann and Jacobi, and with his many pre-critical flirtations with empiricism, ending his ambivalence with respect to the 'Pantheism Controversy' between Jacobi et al. and Mendelssohn et al. Such a claim suggests that the A Deduction, with all of the questions that it raises, is itself a work of ambivalence. Unsure of his ultimate loyalties, Kant walks a tightrope between a notion of an awareness which was not necessarily subjected to consciousness, or, in other words, to a strict, apodeictic self-consciousness, and a commitment to the demands of a unity of apperception and of the authority of reason. However, as we have seen, Kant had evidently decided that these two commitments were incompatible, jettisoning the autonomous phenomenologies of the world in order to preserve his Enlightenment maxim of the authority of reason.

THE GERMAN IDEALIST MOVEMENT

Even during Kant's own lifetime, there emerged a movement in German philosophy which sought to build upon Kant's undeniable and irretrievable advance beyond rationalism and empiricism, but also to respond to his call for a system of transcendental reason. As the tradition unfolded, the movement known as German Idealism has come to be associated with three names: Fichte, Schelling and

Hegel. In this section, I will set out a brief account of the philosophies of each of these thinkers and how each appropriated the
Kantian starting point.

We can most readily understand why German Idealism has been
characterised as a *movement* in light of its spectacular irruption in
the post-Kantian climate at the end of the eighteenth century and
its equally spectacular implosion in the 1830s and 1840s in the wake
of, on the one hand, the *humanist* criticisms of Ludwig Feuerbach
(*The Essence of Christianity*), and, on the other hand, its material-
ist appropriation and transformation in the hands of Karl Marx
(*The Holy Family*, etc.). There remained advocates of each of the
three big names, and Schelling himself continued to stir controversy
into the middle of the nineteenth century, but the specific character
of the German Idealist movement had already lost its integrity by
this time. Hegel himself, despite his untimely demise in the cholera
epidemic of the early 1830s, has had the most enduring legacy of
the three philosophers and continues to this day to be the subject of
growing debate and research. In this section, I will set out a brief
outline of each of these philosophers and of the significance which
each holds in the German Idealist movement.

Fichte, a younger contemporary of Kant who enjoyed an initial
alliance with the great philosopher, sought to erect a system of pure
reason in his main work, *The Science of Knowledge*. The significance
of his philosophy lies in its reliance on the Kantian point of departure and his attempt to defend the standpoint of transcendental idealism in a way which was not merely a repetition of Kant's Critical
Philosophy. Taking as his starting point the 'Copernican
Revolution', Fichte stated that there were two possible standpoints
in philosophy, transcendental idealism and dogmatic empiricism.
The latter, as we have seen, seeks to derive knowledge from the receptivity of the intellect vis-à-vis the objects of experience. The former,
as we have also seen, seeks to disclose the conditions of possibility
for the objects of experience in the transcendental subject. Fichte
held that transcendental idealism was superior to dogmatic empiricism in that it could account for the existence of the object, while the
latter could not. Indeed, Fichte, in the guise of the *logician*, contended that empiricism required an additional, dogmatic assumption of an empirical object, which he called the thing-in-itself (in a
departure from Kant as will be made clear below). Moreover, the
irony of the empiricist standpoint is that it assumes that which

cannot exist and therefore its activity of trying to know the object will always result in futility.

Fichte, for his part, seeks to make the most of Kant's projection of an active consciousness in his view that self-consciousness is a radical striving and is in itself a *pure act*. He takes transcendental idealism to its extreme limit by stating, unashamedly, that the pure ego, or the 'I', is the author of the world. It requires nothing else, and is, from the standpoint of Ockham's razor, able to disclose the truth with the least amount of assumptions. Indeed, he will state that his philosophy rests on no assumptions at all, but only the immediate, *intellectual intuition* of the self in its activity. While a more exhaustive treatment of Fichte goes beyond the present work, suffice it to say that the pure 'I', as self-disclosed in intellectual intuition, posits a non-self, or not-'I', from out of itself. In this way, Fichte begins with self-consciousness, but detects amidst this self-consciousness a consciousness of *otherness* generally. The *place* of this otherness is that which has been already always projected by the pure 'I'. And it is from this originary differentiation between the 'I' and the not-'I' that he articulates a complete philosophy of the world. It is in this way that he follows Kant in his own attempt to lay out the transcendental conditions of possibility of experience in the transcendental subject. In this light, the pure 'I' is the seat and ground of the world as representation, and his philosophy was thus described by Hegel and Marx as 'subjective idealism'. Yet, one could question the feasibility of this starting point since, even though Fichte seeks to set out the entirety of the world from out of his own self, it is clear that there still persists a *remainder* over and above the world created by the self. This is clear in the case of the existence of *raw* matter, which cannot be created by the subject as the latter is responsible only for the formal aspects of existence.

And, while Fichte may say that matter is merely the synthetic combination of space, time and causality (as his one time student Schopenhauer will contend, but in a different context), the suspicion still remains that there persists some primal data upon which consciousness is projected, especially as the self itself is finite and exists within the horizonal limits of necessity, typified most forcefully by death. In this way, the self is not a god, whom Kant defines as that being who needs only to think a thing to have it exist. This is not the case with the self, even if transcendental idealism still holds within the horizons of its own most appropriate limits.

Though he began as a student of Fichte, Schelling soon attempted to distance himself from the pretensions of the absolute, creative 'I', perhaps detecting the same difficulties which I have alluded to in the thematisation of the 'remainder' in Fichte's subjective idealism. At the same time, Schelling, as with each of the German Idealists, sought to set out a system of pure reason, calling his own philosophy an 'Absolute' idealism. Having detected the problematic involved in beginning from the pure Fichtean 'I', Schelling sought to return to the Kantian dual-perspective which sought to disclose the unity and indeed the identity of the ideality of consciousness with the reality of the empirical world (each considered from its own perspective).

Beginning with self-consciousness and with the consciousness of *otherness*, he sought to show how the world or Nature is generated, *à la* Fichte, from the self, but contrary to the latter, how Nature in turn generated the self. There are two series which run side by side, simultaneously, each giving rise to its other (which is distinct from Kant). At the same time, his starting point, in his *System of Transcendental Idealism*, still remains that of self-consciousness.

His own philosophy will undergo its own transformations as he will increasingly begin to question this starting point in the Fichtean self and will move to a philosophy of Nature grounded in an ineffable absolute consciousness which is beyond our knowledge. The roots for this transformation, which will be the central focus of our consideration of his philosophy, can already be detected in his early work in his emphasis upon the *unconscious*, especially as this relates to a proper characterisation of the Kantian *a priori*. Indeed, the questions raised by the notion of the *unconscious* are radical and potentially destructive to the entire Kantian project (as can seen in the philosophy of Nietzsche and in the myriad psychoanalytic appropriations of this latter philosophy by the likes of Freud, Jung, Lacan, Kristeva and Irigaray). For, if the operations of the Kantian *a priori*, or in other words, the projections of time, space and causality are unconscious (as Kant himself seems to suggest when he states that all synthetic activity is rooted in the imagination, the activity of which we are 'barely ever conscious', then the initial delirious feeling of authorial freedom with respect to the web of representations becomes increasingly undermined as we gather that *we* are not in control of this activity. In fact, it may not even be our own.

For, if, in addition to the self-consciousness and consciousness of Kant and Fichte, we also posit the unconscious, then the disconcerting remainder of Fichte breaks out in full force as an *otherness* that may indeed be responsible for the projection of our very selves. In this way, the nexus of experience may not be the projection of our own inherent capacities of mind, but may be the projection of a deeply rooted unconscious that is by definition unknowable to us.

Of course, there is no simple return to the rationalists or empiricists as these latter positions remain on the level of mere consciousness. Yet, Schelling does give us some respite in that what is unknown will slowly unfold in the historicity of our own temporal existence, especially in sublime works of art and in our further understanding of the depths of Nature. But, in this way, we will always remain like Benjamin's 'Angel of History' who is always looking merely to the past.

Hegel, who was a friend of Schelling and who lived with him (and Hölderlin) while he was a student, also recognised the difficulties inherent in a point of departure for philosophy in self-consciousness. He does not deny self-consciousness itself, but sees it not as an *origin*, but as a *result* – it will be the climax to his philosophy of the self-development and unfolding of the 'Concept'. Having characterised Schelling's philosophy as that of 'objective' idealism (apparently forgetting Schelling's post-Fichtean allegiances), he sought to set forth his own version of 'Absolute' idealism, and characterised his approach as a grand synthesis, abolition and transcendence (*Aufhebung*) of Fichte and Schelling. (Cf. the Schelling–Hegel dispute in which the former charged that the latter had stolen his philosophy.)

Instead of beginning with self-consciousness, he begins, as articulated in his *Science of Logic*, with *being* and *nothingness*. In the Preface to this work, he meditates on the difficulty of *any beginning* as he will contend that we are already always amidst the development of being in becoming. His 'beginning' in this way is meant to intimate this embeddedness in becoming, as he writes that being passes over into nothingness and gives rise to *determinant being*, an individuated state of being with limits, with negativity at its heart. From this 'beginning', he lays out, over the next 800 pages, the unfolding of the 'Concept' in all arenas and branches of philosophy and knowledge. The Concept is *thought itself* which explicitly self-differentiates itself into all of its implicit modalities and specifications.

The very movement of this differentiation and unfolding, reminiscent of Aristotle's *Physics* and the notion of *logos* in Heraclitus, is that of contradiction. He sets out the well-known schema of this development in the triad thesis–antithesis–synthesis. Having rejected formal logic, he tells us that we must embrace and *think contradiction* amidst what will become clear, in his *Phenomenology of Spirit*, historicity itself.

The *topos* of his philosophy, and as a sign of his debt to Kant, is temporality, and it could be argued that this temporal unfolding, as it acts in between the polarities of sensibility and understanding, is the transcendental imagination itself. Just as the concept self-differentiates into the entire nexus of thought, history, as it was with Schelling, is the self-disclosure of Reason. However, contrary to Schelling who remained sceptical of our ability to ever comprehend the meaning of existence as we are tied to the unconscious, Hegel maintained a grandiose optimism in claiming that the very goal of history was self-consciousness and Absolute knowledge. Indeed, the goal and end of history is achieved in the self-consciousness of the Absolute Idea, once it has plumbed the depths of its own self-development from the initial movement of being into nothingness.

Hegel's optimism was so grand, in fact, that he stated in his Preface to the *Science of Logic* that the ideas contained in his work were those of 'God before creation'. It was this audacity which earned the ire of Schopenhauer who, as we will see in the following section, was much closer to the pessimism and scepticism of Schelling.

KANT AND SCHOPENHAUER

Schopenhauer, taking his *critical* point of departure from Kant, seeks to indicate the inner truth of existence as the will. The will as the thing-in-itself is not subjected to the principle of sufficient reason. In this way, the will is not determined within the web of representational consciousness, but is the raw striving of existence which will not only not surrender to theoretical or practical reason, but gives rise to the latter as one of its myriad levels of objectification – it is neither the unknown nor the no-thing.

Kant would not like to follow such a path as he is seeking to lay out the groundwork for a *new* metaphysics and would see this Schopenhaurian will as an assertion that violates the limits of possible experience. We can never know anything about the 'X '– which means that theoretical reason can never hope to determine the affairs of practical reason and its *lifeworld*. Of course, this is precisely the criticism by Schopenhauer which plainly states that Kant's conception of the noumena should be 'filled out' by the content of practical existence, and that, if practical reason is to have primacy with respect to theoretical reason, then the status of the intimate apprehension of the will which we call practical reason should not only be raised, but should be granted the possibility of its own type of 'knowing'.

Schopenhauer initially finds this *inside* in the stimulus of the will through intense pleasure or pain in the body, in motivation, and in the basic self-awareness of the mortal being. All of this is a manifestation of the will as it enters the domain of the phenomenon at its differing levels of objectification. Kant however took an anti-metaphysical (from Schopenhauer's perspective) turn with his disclosure of the domain of the will to that of practical reason. We can say almost nothing about the noumena, but, conceived from the perspective of Kant, we can say a lot in a practical manner. There is a differing language for the noumenal dimension, reflecting a differing comportment amidst existence. We have explored this practical, noumenal domain in our consideration of the Second *Critique*.

NEO-KANTIANISM

The emergence of Neo-Kantianism at the turn of the twentieth century briefly maintained a divergent household inhabited by the extremes of such philosophers as Rickert/Heidegger and Carnap/Cohen. The most significant difference lay in the specific interpretation given to the philosophy of Kant in each case. In this context, there is, on the one hand, an epistemological reading of the *Critique of Pure Reason*, which, excepting Cassirer, betrayed a marked disregard for Kant's other Critical works. On the other hand, there is the other interpretation which is concerned with the existence of the finite self amid its world of immediacy, of human existence. One of the points of contention, as we shall see, was the affinity of South-west Neo-Kantianism with the life philosophy of Dilthey. It is in this light that we can begin to comprehend the dissolution of the household. In this way, Neo-Kantianism was a transitionary stage in the history of philosophy which had a significant influence upon the emergence of subsequent and often divergent twentieth-century philosophical movements, such as Logical Positivism, Phenomenology, Critical Theory and Deconstruction.

One of the most important debates in twentieth-century philosophy, which could be argued to be one of the founding events in the current division of philosophy in the current era, began from certain decisions on the significance of the Kantian Philosophy. This debate erupted in Germany in the late 1920s between two schools of philosophy, that of the Marburg School and the South-west German School. It is important to note at the outset that this debate did not remain a merely German affair, but has spilled over to the many nations of Europe (including the United Kingdom) and throughout the world.

The main proponents of the former school were Cohen, Cassirer and Carnap, those of the latter, Rickert and Heidegger (although the latter himself spent a decade in Marburg). What is significant in this debate was the common point of departure in Kantian philosophy. The debate, of course, hinged on the specific appropriations of the Kantian philosophy for each 'camp'.

Friedman and Gabriel have explored the various controversies surrounding what they see as the root of the current 'divide' in philosophy. In their respective analyses, we can see two distinct positions emerge which, for good or ill, are still with us. On the one hand, the Marburg School set out a distinctly *epistemological* interpretation of the philosophy of Kant, disregarding to a large extent his Second and Third *Critiques* with a focus upon the 'theory of knowledge' which, in their interpretation, Kant developed in the *Critique of Pure Reason*. (N.B. Cassirer is an exception in this dispute as he decisively moved away from this school in the elaboration of his *Philosophy of Symbolic Forms.*) In this way, the Marburg School was interested in deploying Kant as an authority for their contention that philosophy was to become an adjunct to the natural sciences (*Naturwissenschaften*).

And, on the other hand, the South-west German School, based in Freiburg, with Heidegger being the most significant exponent, would insist that Kant's work had an entirely different significance (while not denying its routine epistemological components), setting out an interpretation of the Kantian philosophy which, bringing in the entirety of his Critical Project, emphasised the new grounding of metaphysics which Kant was developing and its impact upon an exploration of human existence. This analysis was, therefore, oriented to a significant concern for the human sciences (*Geisteswissenschaften*), one not merely concerned with questions of knowledge and logic, but also with metaphysics, ethics and aesthetics.

A major flashpoint in this debate was that between Heidegger and Carnap. The former set forth a novel interpretation of 'metaphysics' in his Inaugural Lecture for his Professorship of Philosophy, 'What is Metaphysics?', at the University of Freiburg in 1929. Setting out from his own (post-) Neo-Kantian framework, which was admixed with the 'Life Philosophies' of Wilhelm Dilthey, Friedrich Nietzsche and Søren Kierkegaard, Heidegger explored the question of *transcendence* as the condition of possibility of human existence and knowledge. He pitched his address through an explication of that which he indicated as the 'nothing' – or as we have come to understand it, the 'no-thing' (cf. his mention of Hegel in the first paragraph of his Address).

His main contention was that while science explored that which *is*, as a *something*, there always remains the residual question of *that which is not*, or beyond the limits of the 'thing'. He further contended that this 'not' was not merely the negated object of the scientific proposition, of the logical negation of the intellect, but was, as he eventually disclosed in his Address, a transcendental condition of possibility of existence which disclosed the basic temporal root of being-human.

This, indeed, calls to mind the distinction which we will explore again below between the *phenomenon* and the *noumena* in the Kantian philosophy, between *sensibility*, the conditioned object of representation, of experience, and the *intelligible*, the transcendental ground of the possibility of experience. In this light, what Heidegger attempts to articulate is that which lies at the limits of the labyrinth of representative knowledge, not as an 'outside' about which we must remain silent, but as a *root* which discloses the possibility of differing *topologies*, or regions, of truth, each of which must have its own specific modality of expression. Yet, more importantly, for Heidegger, each science constitutes, following Husserl, a regional phenomenology which must have its own ways and means of disclosure, and thus, its own criteria of rigour, truth and meaning.

That there exists something beyond the *something* of standard science, that there is a *before* and *beyond* of the nexus of representation, in the epistemological sense of knowledge, necessitates that we consider philosophy in the broader sense of a phenomenology of regional topologies rooted in the temporality of human existence. But, this is, again, merely the Kantian move of taking a step back from the empirical fact and asking the question, 'Why?'.

Carnap, who was deeply influenced by the *early* Wittgenstein (although the latter himself repudiated his own earlier work and that of logical positivism), attacked Heidegger's Inaugural Address in his 1931 essay, 'The Elimination of Metaphysics Through Logical Analysis of Language'. While it is generally agreed that Carnap neither read nor sought to understand Heidegger's philosophy, the position he sets out is interesting as he himself also takes his point of departure from 'Kant'. And his position, that of *logical positivism*, is important as we seek to understand Kant from our own specific situation in the *historicity* of philosophy.

Carnap, emerging from the reduced epistemological tradition of Marburg Neo-Kantianism, sought to define philosophy as an exercise which would 'clean up' the pursuit of truth into a mere clarification of the truth claims of natural science. He defined an analytic criterion of application which included a dual commitment to a logical criterion of analysis and an empirical verification of truth claims, both consistent, it would seem, with the first one hundred pages or so of Kant's *Critique of Pure Reason*. In other words, he regarded knowledge as a combination of sensation (empirical verification) and formal logic, which is one way to interpret Kant, although it is not clear if his conception of logic is consistent with Kant's notion of a *transcendental* logic of the conditions of possibility of experience. For Carnap, if a verbal utterance or written text did not satisfy this criterion, even if it satisfied historical and grammatical senses of meaning and significance, it would still to be deemed philosophically *meaningless*. It was from this standpoint that Carnap attacked Heidegger's Inaugural Address, and, indeed, the metaphysical philosophies of the German Idealists, as instances of *meaningless* 'metaphysics'. In fact, he mentions them by name.

In his essay, Carnap attacks Heidegger for his use of the term 'nothing' as a noun, disregarding this usage as an indication of transcendence. From his perspective, such a usage violates the criterion of application in the sense of empirical verifiability (unless 'nothing' is meant in the psychological sense of *angst* which he decides is not the case from his analysis of Heidegger's text). He writes that any meaningful sense of the word 'nothing' must be that of logical negation. Heidegger, anticipating the entirety of Carnap's onslaught, himself states in his Address that the use of this term will incite, from the perspective of science, the cry of the absurd.

While we will not resolve this dispute here, it is interesting that both of the parties rely on a Kantian starting point. As I have suggested, Carnap sets out the elements of sensation and formal logic in his criteria of application. For him, Heidegger transcends the conditions of possibility of experience. Yet, at the same time, Heidegger himself claims to be articulating these very conditions as he sets out the *nothing*, or the no-thing, as the condition of possibility for experience, in this case, the condition for the possibility of scientific experience. It is interesting, in this way, that these two radically different philosophies can set out from a common point of departure. And it is a testament to the philosophy of Kant that there can be such myriad interpretations of a seemingly inexhaustible text.

THE CONTINENTAL/ANALYTIC DIVIDE

I have explored the dispute between Heidegger and Carnap because it is not only indicative of the *hermeneutical* possibilities of the Kantian text, but also still has a major significance for philosophy today, in the context of the Continental/Analytic divide. While there are other disputes, debates, and names (not to mention the divisions within the Continental and Analytic philosophies themselves), this controversy exposes a basic conflict of which the student of European philosophy must be aware. It is through a comprehension of the historicity of one's own situation, after all, that one will be able to 'think for oneself'.

It is clear that Kant has had a major influence upon both sides of this divide, but this influence, as we have seen, is quite varied and complex, giving rise to entirely new philosophies in the nineteenth and twentieth centuries. What is perhaps most significant about the Neo-Kantianism of Carnap and his associates is their attempt to set forth a *restricted* interpretation of the First *Critique*. As I have suggested, this interpretation lays out two essential aspects for 'authentic' knowledge, formal logic and empirical verification. Of course, it would be quite easy to find such threads in the work of Kant. There are after all many discussions of logic and of the fallacies of reason, as we saw for instance in the section on the

KANT'S *CRITIQUE OF PURE REASON*

Amphiboly, and in the Transcendental Dialectic. However, there is not only much more to Kant's text than this restricted use, there are also extensive examples of philosophers who have set forth readings of Kant in an entirely different spirit. This is clear of European philosophers from the German Idealists, through Heidegger and Arendt, to philosophers of our own era such as Deleuze, Habermas and Henry Allison.

It is not clear if a logical and epistemological interpretation of Kant is resonant with the philosophical workings of the Critical Philosophy which does not primarily concern formal logic, but rather a transcendental logic. Indeed, formal logic merely stands as a contrast in the exposition of Kant's *new metaphysics*. Likewise, it is not possible to remain faithful to Kant if his other *Critiques* are not brought into play, as they are in the First *Critique*. Issues of ethics and aesthetics do belong to philosophy for Kant, and their discourses are meaningful. Perhaps the real difference between Continental and Analytic philosophy lies precisely in a disagreement with respect to the *meaning of meaning*. For the former, as with Kant himself, meaning to a large extent is context dependent. A word used in a theoretical context will have an entirely different meaning or sense in the context of the practical. Moreover, Continental philosophy seeks to broaden the possibilities of meaning and of the hermeneutical possibilities for the attainment of knowledge. For the Analytic philosopher, on the contrary, Kant's contribution is to be judged by the tribunal of the Analytic revolution, its anti-metaphysical agenda, and its programme of logical and linguistic reductionism. There is little interest in not only Kant's other works, but also in the more intriguing questions intimated by his work, questions explored by those post-Kantian philosophers who are now part of the tradition of European Philosophy.

In fact, not only did the logical positivists (and their heirs) appropriate the philosophy of Kant according to their own interests and theoretical protocols, but they, as Carnap shows quite openly, have sought to criticise and exclude from the domain of meaningfulness (philosophy) most or all of the post-Kantian philosophers who did dare to read Kant in a different way, such as the German Idealists, Schopenhauer, Hegel, and most obviously Heidegger. In light of such incommensurate readings of Kant, it would be difficult to decide our next step. However, Kant's concept of community may shed some light on our dilemma.

This concept is based upon a disjunctive judgment which separates and at once unites the disparate members of a community. Such was the strategy with respect to the community of human knowledge which necessitated the disjunction between the theoretical and the practical. However, Kant warns of the possibility that one of the members may wish to eliminate the other, taking control of the entire community. This attempt was made, we can suggest, in Carnap's dogmatism. However, Kant suggests that such an attempt is a transgression of one's own most proper realm, and that such a transgressor must be criticised and brought back into the discipline of reason. It is not clear, however, if there exists any tribunal which could enforce the demands of reason. Of course, the philosophical 'community' as a whole could be such a discourse which could seek to maintain the integrity of the differing typologies of philosophy and the different regions of truth. Yet, this will not be done only in the manner of Kant, through criticism. For, as is clear from his influence, Kant has opened up a vast and varied terrain of philosophical exploration and questioning that is already *on its way*. Most Continental or European philosophy can directly or indirectly trace their lineage to Kant or one of the post-Kantians. And, these philosophies still exist and will continue to exist – they will not be eliminated by the logical analysis of language. In this way, it is through philosophical creativity that the best criticism is enacted.

The divide between Continental and Analytic philosophy can perhaps be explained by the fact that, on the one hand, having dismissed outright most or all of European philosophy, the latter has not attempted to engage in any constructive or truly critical engagement with that philosophy. On the other hand, having been dismissed so violently, European philosophers have simply cleared their own space and have continued to investigate philosophers who have been deemed 'meaningless'. There has been little reason or opportunity, until quite recently, to have it any other way. Perhaps Kant's description of the 'natural dialectic of reason' may be illuminating in relation to this question. As we have seen, reason inevitably asks questions which have no answer. But, we will still ask the questions. From this perspective alone, the Analytic revolution could have been more circumspect. Yet, it would be a gross mistake to regard Continental philosophers as those who deal only in the 'figments of the brain'. Indeed, Carnap is not the only one to have read his Kant and to have cultivated philosophical rigour and the critical instinct.

Continental philosophy has its own critical and deconstructive protocols and is well versed in the mis-use of language. However, once again, it is the context and an openness to various regions of philosophical questioning, including that of the historical, which distinguishes the latter from Analytic philosophy. Of course, in light of the growing impression that the Analytic revolution has stalled (and the equally growing sense that there has now been a resurgence of interest in Continental philosophy for forty years), there is much room for movement and repositionings across the *topos* of Philosophy.

Yet, as Kant and Heidegger have pointed out (as well as almost every major European philosopher since Kant) there is a basic disjunction between logic and experience, especially if the latter is conceived in a transcendental manner. We are still caught in the battle between Frege and Dilthey, between logic and life, and it is not clear if any authentic community can arise from this fundamental disjunction.

NOTES

1 Immanuel Kant, 'What is Enlightenment?' in *Perpetual Peace and Other Essays*, Trs. Ted Humphrey, Indianapolis: Hackett Publishing Company, 1983, p. 41.
2 Kant, *Inaugural Dissertation: On the Form and Principle of the Sensible and Intelligible World*, New York: AMS Press, 1970, pp. 45–6.
3 For instance, we have the well known statement that he is seeking to *limit theoretical reason in order to make room for faith* and his seminal distinction between phenomenon and noumena (as already indicated in the *Inaugural Dissertation*). There is also the sustained discussion of the free dimension of reason, and, as we will see in our overview of the *Critique of Practical Reason*, the notion of a causality of freedom, even if only negatively postulated in the Third Antinomy of the Transcendental Dialectic. And, beyond this quite novel dialectic of reason, Kant also offers us a 'Canon of Pure Reason' in Division Two, 'The Transcendental Doctrine of the Elements'.
4 Heidegger, Martin. *Being and Time*, Trs. John Macquarrie & Edward Robinson, New York: Harper & Row Publishers, 1962. Cf. also Tillich, Paul. *The Courage to Be*, New Haven: Yale University Press, 1980, p. 142 ff.
5 This is a provisional reference to Waxman's *Kant's Model of the Mind*.
6 For a contemporary re-reading of the philosophy of Leibniz, see Luchte, 'Mathesis and Analysis: Finitude and the Infinite in the *Monadology* of Leibniz', *Heythrop Journal*, 2006.
7 I do not wish to confine Kant to this single metaphor, since there are clearly others operative throughout the text, such as the building metaphor and that involving a spring of water. It is the 'root' metaphor which would play such a central role in Heidegger's interpretation of Kant.
8 A 82, B108: 'If we have the original and primitive concepts, it is easy to add the derivative and subsidiary, and so to give a complete picture of the family tree of the concepts of pure understanding'.
9 Compare A121: 'If however representations reproduced one another in any order just as they happened to come together, this would not lead to any determinate connection of them, but only to accidental collocations; and so would not give rise to any knowledge'.

10 Cf. Nietzsche's parody of this pathos of reason (ratio) in *Beyond Good and Evil*, Aph. 2:

> How could something originate in its antithesis? Truth in error, for example? Or will to truth in will to deception? Or the unselfish act in self-interest? Or the pure radiant gaze of the sage in covetousness? Such origination is impossible; he who dreams of it is a fool, indeed worse than a fool; the things of the highest value must have another origin of their own: they cannot be derivable from this transitory, seductive, deceptive, mean little world, from this confusion of desire and illusion! In the womb of being, rather, in the intransitory, in the hidden god, in the 'things-in-itself' – that is where their cause must lie and nowhere else!

11 This is implied in the A Deduction despite the undertow of the logical identity, and hence, ultimacy of the apperceptive act.

12 Kant writes at A120: 'There must therefore exist in us an active faculty for the synthesis of this manifold. To this faculty I give the title, imagination. Its action, when directed upon perceptions, I entitle apprehension. Since imagination has to bring the manifold of intuition into the form of an image, it must previously have taken the impressions up into its activity, that is, have apprehended them.' Also in a note at A121: 'Psychologists have hitherto failed to realise that imagination is a necessary ingredient of perception itself.'

13 The metaphor of vision and blindness in the A Deduction, a metaphor which is not present in the B Deduction, implies at least a duality between imagination and understanding, as vision implies distance between the viewer and the viewed. The B Deduction, on the other hand, abandons the metaphor of blindness since it fails to distinguish the imagination from the understanding, and thus, remove any distance which would allow for a detachment of the faculties with respect to their principles of composition.

14 The undeniable discrepancies which exist between the A and B Deductions indicate a point of susceptibility of the Kantian text to the destruction performed by Heidegger, with his emphasis upon the 'phenomenological' deduction carried out in the A Edition.

15 This once again underlines Kant's overriding logical criteria which proscribe the significance of the ontological questions which arise in the avenue of the imagination.

16 Compare this to A125 in the A Deduction which lists the empirical employments of imagination 'in recognition, reproduction, association, and apprehension'. It is the imagination which acts in this scenario, but acts according to the rules of apperception. In the B Deduction, responding to the charges of Berkeleyan idealism, to the attacks upon reason by Jacobi and Hamann, and to criticisms of his style, Kant takes his position to its logical conclusion. He was therefore willing to sacrifice the dignity of the creative and transcendental imagination in order to save his notion of truth.

17 With respect to the clarification of the ground to the threefold synthesis in the A Deduction, we could answer that each, in its own way, is the ground, one in terms of generation, the other in terms of outcome. This of course is distinct from the question of the legitimacy of the concept

to command the imagination, or in what amounts to the same thing, whether or not the imagination is truly in need of the unity of the concept.

18 Furthermore, the reproductive imagination, which in the A Deduction, was described as a 'transcendental act of the mind', is relegated in the B Deduction to the domain of psychology.

19 However, Kant does not thereby overthrow formal logic, but encloses it within its own domain of purity. This 'purism' of the laws of logic (and thus of reason, which cannot relate to objects) was an absurdity for some of Kant's contemporaries and has become a problem for many subsequent inquirers, Heidegger among them. It could be suggested however that the emphasis on the exclusion of logic in its formal sense from 'centre stage' shows a continuity with the A Deduction and not with the B Deduction which brings logic to the foreground in the same movement which diminishes imagination.

20 I would have preferred to write 'negotiation', but it is difficult conceiving of a negotiation which is working toward a 'subsumption', except in a negotiation of surrender or annexation. Yet, such a hierarchial relationship conflicts with the lip-service Kant gives to the lack of precedence among the faculties. This claim is obviously not true, and Kant's entire project is a history of the conflict between reciprocity and logical precedence.

21 Note the stylistic continuity of this passage with the A Deduction, and not with the usage of the B Deduction. For Kant does not write that the schema is a product of the understanding, under the title of imagination, but a product of the imagination.

22 Kant justifies the subjection, or effective containment of the imagination to the principle of the unity of apperception when he contrasts the works of imagination with the ideal of reason in what could be described as a prejudicial, but consistent remark:

> Such is the nature of the ideal of reason, which must always rest on determinate concepts and serve as a rule and archetype, alike in our actions and in our critical judgments. The products of the imagination are of an entirely different nature; no one can explain or give an intelligible concept of them; each is a kind of monogram, a mere set of particular qualities, determined by no assignable rule, and forming rather a blurred sketch drawn from diverse experience than a determinate image – a representation such as painters and physiognomists profess to carry in their heads, and which they treat as being an incommunicable shadowy image of their creations or even of their critical judgments. (A570–71, B598)

Thus containment can be considered as expressing no more than the harnessing of the results of the power of imagination by means of the cognitive (and not the operational) principle of the unity of apperception. What becomes clear is the narrow notion of truth that is allowed by Kant's conception of *a priori* knowledge, which we can fathom from his own allegory of an island of truth amid the stormy ocean of darkness threatening on all sides. (A235, B294)

23 In 'The Discipline of Pure Reason' (A770, B798) he writes, acknowledging tacitly that he must remain blind to other visions:

> If the imagination is not simply to be visionary, but is to be inventive under the strict surveillance of reason, there must always previously be something that is completely certain, and not invented or merely a matter of opinion, namely the possibility of the object itself.

24 The issue of the status of the imagination with respect to its independence is another way of considering the separability of the concept from the determination by the imagination by means of the limits inherent in possible experience, or existence. At stake is the possibility of a plurivocity of truth, or truths without the hierarchisation inherent in the Kantian architectonic.

25 See Beiser, *The Fate of Reason*, pp. 266–284.

26 It was actually Hamann who, as an older contemporary of Kant, and a major influence upon Goethe, Herder, Schelling, etc., first introduced Kant to not only Hume, but also Rousseau.

27 Categories which will not fit with the criteria of subordination are: substance and accidents, since the accidents are the mode of life of the substance itself; community, which is a mere aggregate and not a series; the concepts of modality, as none of them forms a series. The category of relation that does fit with the cosmological ideas is that of causality whose very essence seems to form a series of subordination.

28 Cf. Luchte, 'Mathesis and Analysis: Finitude and the Infinite in the *Monadology* of Leibniz', *Heythrop Journal*, 2006

29 Beiser, *The Fate of Reason*.

GUIDE TO FURTHER READING

Translations
Kant, Immanuel. (1965) *Critique of Pure Reason*, Trs. by N. K. Smith, New York: St. Martin's Press.
—— (1970) *Inaugural Dissertation: On the Form and Principle of the Sensible and the Intelligible World* (1770). Trs. By W. J. Eckoff, New York: AMS Press.
—— (1996) *Critique of Practical Reason*, Trs. by T. K. Abbott, New York: Prometheus Books.
—— (1951) *Critique of Judgment*, Trs. by J. H. Bernard, New York: Hafner Press.
—— (1960) *Religion Within the Limits of Reason Alone*, Trs. by Theodore M. Greene & Hoyt H. Hudson, New York: Harper Torchbooks.
Fichte, J. G. (1991) *The Science of Knowledge*, Trs. by Peter Heath and John Lachs, New York: Cambridge University Press.
Schelling, F. W. J. (2001) *System of Transcendental Logic*, Trs. by Peter Heath, Charlottesville: University Press of Virginia.
Hegel, G. W. F. (1987) *Logic*, Trs. by William Wallace, Oxford: Clarendon Press.

References and Further Reading
Allison, H. (1983) *Kant's Transcendental Idealism*, New Haven: Yale University Press.
—— (1990) *Kant's Theory of Freedom*, Cambridge: Cambridge University Press.
Arendt, H. (1982) *Lectures on Kant's Political Philosophy*, R. Beiner (ed.), Chicago: University of Chicago Press.
Atterton, P. (2001), 'From Transcendental Freedom to the Other: Levinas and Kant', *In Proximity: Emmanuel Levinas and the Eighteenth Century*, M. New, R. Bernasconi and R. Cohen (eds), Lubbock: Texas Tech University Press, 327–354.
Bataille, G. (1988) *Inner Experience*, Trs. by L.A. Boldt, Albany: SUNY Press.

Bataille, G. (1992) *Theory of Religion*, Trs. R. Hurley, New York: Zone Books.

Beiser, F. (1987) *The Fate of Reason*, Harvard: Harvard University Press.

Cassirer, E. (1981) *Kant's Life and Thought*, Trs. by James Haden, Yale: Yale University Press.

Deleuze, G. (1984) *Kant's Critical Philosophy*, Trs. by H. Tomlinson and B. Habberjam, London, Athlone Press.

Friedman, M. (2000) *A Parting of the Ways: Carnap, Cassirer, and Heidegger*, LaSalle:Open Court Publishing.

Gabriel, G. (2003) 'Carnap's "Elimination of Metaphysics Through Logical Analysis of Language". A Retrospective Consideration of the Relationship between Continental and Analytic Philosophy', *Logical Empiricism: Historical and Contemporary Perspectives*, Paolo Parrini, Wesley C. Salmon, Marrilee H.Salmon (eds), Pittsburgh: Pittsburgh University Press.

Gardner, S. (1999) *Kant and the Critique of Pure Reason*, London: Routledge.

Guyer, P. (1987) *Kant and the Claims of Knowledge*, Cambridge: CUP.

Heidegger, M. (1997) *Phenomenological Interpretation of Kant's Critique of Pure Reason*. Indiana: Indiana University Press.

—— (1997) *Kant and the Problem of Metaphysics*, Trs. by Richard Taft, Indiana:Indiana University Press.

Husserl, E. (1971) *The Phenomenology of Internal Time-Consciousness*, M. Heidegger (ed.), Indiana: Indiana University Press.

Levinas, E. (1998) *Otherwise than Being, Or Beyond Essence*, Trs. by A. Lingus, Pittsburgh: Duquesne University Press.

Luchte, J. (2006) 'Mathesis and Analysis: Finitude and the Infinite in the *Monadology* of Leibniz', *Heythrop Journal*, Vol. 47, No. 4.

Lyotard, J. (1994) *Lessons on the Analytic of the Sublime*, Trs. by Elizabeth Rottenberg, Palo Alto: Stanford University Press.

Makreel, R. (1990) *Imagination and Interpretation in Kant: The Hermeneutical Import of the Critique of Judgment*, Chicago: University of Chicago Press.

Nietzsche, F. (1996) *Philosophy in the Tragic Age of the Greeks*, Trs. by Marianne Cowan, Washington: Regnery Publishing.

Rockmore, T. (2006) *In Kant's Wake: Philosophy in the Twentieth Century*, Oxford: Blackwell Publishing.

Schopenhauer, A. (1969) *The World as Will and Representation*, Vol. 1, Trs. by E.F.J. Payne, New York: Dover Publications.

Schürmann, R. (2003) *Broken Hegemonies*, Trs. by R. Lilly, Indiana: Indiana University Press.

Smith, Norman Kemp. (2003) *A Commentary on Kant's Critique of Pure Reason*, New York: Palgrave Macmillan.

Waxman, W. (2005) *Kant and the Empiricists*, Oxford: Oxford University Press.

—— (1991) *Kant's Model of the Mind: A New Interpretation of Transcendental Idealism*, Oxford: Oxford University Press.

Zammito, J. (1992) *The Genesis of Kant's Critique of Judgment*, Chicago: University of Chicago Press.

Žižek, S. (1999) 'The Deadlock of Transcendental Imagination', in *The Ticklish Subject*, New York: Verso Press.

Kant Resources and Links

http://etext.library.adelaide.edu.au/k/kant/immanuel
The University of Adelaide – Kant e-books

http://www.hkbu.edu.hk/~ppp/K1tools.html
Kant on the Web

http://www.gutenberg.org/etext/4280
Kant: Critique of Pure Reason – Project Gutenberg

http://www.deistnet.com/crpracrn.txt
Kant: Critique of Practical Reason

http://www.deistnet.com/crjudgmt.txt
Kant: Critique of Judgement

http://www.deistnet.com/relreson.txt
Kant: Religion Within the Limits of Reason Alone

http://people.brandeis.edu/~teuber/textsonline.html
Philosophy Texts Online

http://www.constitution.org/kant/perpeace.htm
Kant: Perpetual Peace</a>

http://www.hkbu.edu.hk/~ppp/KR.html
The Kantian Review

http://hcl.harvard.edu/research/guides/philosophy
Philosophy Resources at Harvard

http://naks.ucsd.edu
North American Kant Society

http://www.nobunaga.demon.co.uk/htm/kant.htm
Immanuel Kant Room

http://plato.stanford.edu/entries/kant-development
Kant's Philosophical Development

http://www.swan.ac.uk/poli/texts/kant/kantcon.htm
Kant: Groundwork for the Metaphysics of Morals

http://www.unc.edu/~jfr/Texts/Kantlit6.htm
Critique of Pure Reason Resources

http://www.opendemocracy.net/conflict/article_1749.jsp
Immanuel Kant and the Iraq War – Roger Scruton

http://www.phil.upenn.edu/~cubowman/fichte
North American Fichte Society

http://radicalacademy.com/philfichte.htm
The Philosophy of Johann Gottlieb Fichte

http://www.marxists.org/reference/subject/philosophy/works/ge/schellin.htm
Schelling's System of Transcendental Philosophy (Introduction)

http://www.uwp.co.uk/book_desc/kant.html
The Kantian Review (UK)

http://www.epistemelinks.com/Main/Philosophers.aspx?PhilCode=Kant
Episteme Links – Kant

http://ethics.sandiego.edu/theories/Kant/index.asp
Kant and Kantian Ethics – Ethics Updates

http://humanum.arts.cuhk.edu.hk/Philosophy/Kant/cpr/
Kant's Critique of Pure Reason – Norman Kemp Smith translation

http://www.english.upenn.edu/~mgamer/Etexts/kant.html
Kant – 'What is Enlightenment?'

APPENDIX: CONTENTS OF THE *CRITIQUE OF PURE REASON WITH A & B LOCATIONS*

The Canon of Pure Reason
(NKS 630; A797/B825)
The Architectonic of Pure Reason
(NKS 653; A832/B860)
The History of Pure Reason
(NKS 666; A852/B880)

INDEX

66874728R00114

Made in the USA
Lexington, KY
27 August 2017